Has Trust in the U.S. Intelligence Community Eroded?

Examining the Relationship Between Policymakers and Intelligence Providers

CHRISTOPHER DICTUS, YULIYA SHOKH, ISABELLE NAZHA, MAREK N. POSARD, RICHARD S. GIRVEN, SINA BEAGHLEY, ANTHONY VASSALO

Prepared for the Office of the Secretary of Defense
Approved for public release; distribution is unlimited

NATIONAL SECURITY RESEARCH DIVISION

For more information on this publication, visit **www.rand.org/t/RRA864-1**.

About RAND

The RAND Corporation is a research organization that develops solutions to public policy challenges to help make communities throughout the world safer and more secure, healthier and more prosperous. RAND is nonprofit, nonpartisan, and committed to the public interest. To learn more about RAND, visit www.rand.org.

Research Integrity

Our mission to help improve policy and decisionmaking through research and analysis is enabled through our core values of quality and objectivity and our unwavering commitment to the highest level of integrity and ethical behavior. To help ensure our research and analysis are rigorous, objective, and nonpartisan, we subject our research publications to a robust and exacting quality-assurance process; avoid both the appearance and reality of financial and other conflicts of interest through staff training, project screening, and a policy of mandatory disclosure; and pursue transparency in our research engagements through our commitment to the open publication of our research findings and recommendations, disclosure of the source of funding of published research, and policies to ensure intellectual independence. For more information, visit www.rand.org/about/principles.

RAND's publications do not necessarily reflect the opinions of its research clients and sponsors.

Published by the RAND Corporation, Santa Monica, Calif.
© 2024 RAND Corporation
RAND® is a registered trademark.

Library of Congress Cataloging-in-Publication Data is available for this publication.

ISBN: 978-1-9774-1277-5

Cover: Golubovy/Adobe Stock, graphic courtesy of the Office of the Director of National Intelligence.

About This Report

Media reports and articles by policy and U.S. Intelligence Community (IC) professionals over the past several years have suggested that the IC is held in increasingly lower regard by some decisionmakers—and also by some groups in the general citizenry—and that predictions made by some IC professionals have had variable success in influencing decisionmakers over time. We explored whether and to what degree trust in intelligence predictions and national estimates has been degraded over time and what internal and external factors might drive any perceived or real bias, inequity, or change. We also explored any change in or degradation of the relationship between policymakers and the IC over time, mapping the causes, consequences, and historical genesis over multiple presidential administrations.

The research reported here was completed in December 2021 and underwent security review with the sponsor and the Defense Office of Prepublication and Security Review before public release.

RAND National Security Research Division

This research was sponsored by the Office of the Secretary of Defense and conducted within the International Security and Defense Policy Program of the RAND National Security Research Division (NSRD), which operates the National Defense Research Institute (NDRI), a federally funded research and development center sponsored by the Office of the Secretary of Defense, the Joint Staff, the Unified Combatant Commands, the Navy, the Marine Corps, the defense agencies, and the defense intelligence enterprise.

For more information on the RAND International Security and Defense Policy Program, see www.rand.org/nsrd/isdp or contact the director (contact information is provided on the webpage).

Acknowledgments

We would like to thank Michael McNerney for his support of this project. We are grateful to all the intelligence leaders and policymakers who participated in this study and who generously shared their time and perspectives with us. Thank you to our reviewers, Michael Decker and Karen Sudkamp, for their careful read and helpful comments, which clarified our analysis and helped improve the overall quality of this report.

Summary

Issue

Over the past several years, media reports and articles by policy and U.S. Intelligence Community (IC) professionals have suggested that the IC is held in increasingly lower regard by some decisionmakers—and also by some in the general public—and that predictions made by IC professionals have had variable success in influencing decisionmakers. We explored whether and to what degree trust in intelligence predictions and national estimates has been degraded over time and what internal and external factors might be drivers of any perceived or real changes in the relationship between policymakers and the IC.

Approach

In 2020 and 2021, we conducted 11 interviews with current and former U.S. intelligence leaders and policymakers whose careers spanned multiple administrations. The team asked about (1) these leaders' direct experience with intelligence estimates, (2) potential bias in intelligence or policymaking, and (3) specific examples of internal or external bias that they witnessed or of which they were aware.[1] We reviewed historical literature and analyses of suspected bias in or influence on intelligence processes, descriptions of intelligence "failures," memoirs of senior officials, and other literature to identify any instances of bias or influence that altered estimates or assessments. Finally, we analyzed the interviews and literature for themes related

---

[1] We submitted requisite information to the RAND National Security Research Division's Human Subjects Protection Committee screener in September 2020 and received a determination that "No further review is required and you may proceed with your study." Therefore, Human Subjects Protection protocols have been used in this report in accordance with the appropriate statutes and U.S. Department of Defense (DoD) regulations governing Human Subjects Protection. All interviews were anonymized, and names were kept separate from interview notes. These sources' views are solely their own and do not represent the official policy or position of DoD or the U.S. government.

to trust—or the lack thereof—in the IC in general and in the relationship that existed between the IC and policymakers across several administrations. With regard to the interviews and historical events we analyzed, we recognize that each individual spoke from the position from which they observed the event. Therefore, in this report, we summarize those viewpoints, put them in historical context, and call out similarities in observations between interviews where they exist, but we also recognize that there may well be counterpoints and varying views of how events unfolded and about the motivations behind individual actions depending on the position from which an individual observed or participated in the process.

Across our exploratory review of the literature, which focused on public trust (or distrust) of, public attitudes toward, and bias within the IC, we found extensive literature that hinted at or spoke directly to internal or external biases. Using our initial results, we shifted to a systematic review, developing search strings that retrieved 211 English language, peer-reviewed articles from two popular databases, Scopus and Web of Science, between 1988 and 2021. We then reviewed the abstracts of these articles and identified 51 that relate to the IC. We excluded articles that focused on foreign intelligence communities (e.g., in the Soviet Union) or topics unrelated to trust and the IC (e.g., political party structures in states). Our final sample was 51 articles. In Appendix C, we describe the details of our search strategy and discuss the limitations of this study.

Conclusions

After analyzing the literature and the interview texts, we arrived at several conclusions. First, the degree of perceived bias in intelligence estimates is highly dependent on the presidential administration in power. Second, policymakers most frequently introduce bias in intelligence assessments from a desire to minimize the appearance of dissent. Third, the IC tends to introduce bias through self-censorship—the IC tries to either maintain its relevance and utility or avoid the ire of policymakers. Finally, we observed tensions in the relationship between IC professionals and policymakers: The IC has an incentive to elicit positive feedback from policymakers, and there are limited benefits (with regard to both the careers of intelligence professionals and their agencies' budgets) in receiving negative feedback from policymakers. These tensions could create friction between (1) providing objective information and analysis to policymakers and (2) serving policymakers as customers of intelligence. Thus, it appears that the IC is motivated to be "not wrong" more than it is motivated to be right in its predictions.

Contents

Table

CHAPTER ONE

Introduction and Approach

This exploratory study was initiated during the administration of President Donald Trump, when extensive media reports and articles suggested that the U.S. Intelligence Community (IC) was held in increasingly low regard by the President and some of his senior administration officials.[1] During informal conversations with some intelligence officials serving at the time, RAND Corporation researchers heard stories about low morale and perceptions of a disregard of intelligence analysis by the Trump administration. Researchers also heard stories about some instances of the administration ignoring truth in favor of information that supported its policies. Reputable media reports further substantiated these views.[2]

These stories caused the project team to wonder whether disregard of U.S. intelligence by administrations was a new phenomenon or whether it had been present for some time and was merely increasing in intensity (and whether public awareness about it was increasing). RAND researchers explored (1) whether and to what degree trust in intelligence predictions and national estimates has degraded over time and (2) what internal and external factors might be drivers of any perceived or real bias, inequity, or analytic process change in the evaluation of evidence by either the IC

---

[1] See Chapter Eight on the Trump administration for a more detailed discussion of these media reports and interviews.

[2] Some examples of these media reports are Robert Draper, "Unwanted Truths: Inside Trump's Battle with U.S. Intelligence Agencies," *New York Times*, August 25, 2020; Mary Louise Kelly, "A History of Trump's Broken Ties to the U.S. Intelligence Community," *All Things Considered*, October 28, 2019; and Michael Morell, Avril Haines, and David S. Cohen, "Trump's Politicization of U.S. Intelligence Agencies Could End in Disaster," *Foreign Policy*, April 28, 2020.

or policymakers. Specifically, we explored any change in or degradation of estimative processes over time and changes in relationships between the IC and policymakers over multiple presidential administrations.

Approach

Across our exploratory review of the literature, which focused on public trust or distrust of, public attitudes toward, and bias within the IC, we found extensive sources that hinted at or spoke directly to internal or external biases. After our initial search, we validated our results by conducting a systematic literature review. We developed search strings that retrieved 211 English-language, peer-reviewed articles from two popular databases, Scopus and Web of Science, between 1988 and 2021. We then reviewed the abstracts of these articles and identified the final sample of 51 articles that related to the IC. We excluded articles that focused on foreign intelligence communities (e.g., in the Soviet Union) or topics that are unrelated to trust and the IC (e.g., political party structures in states). In Appendix C, we describe the details of our search strategy and discuss the limitations of this study.

In 2020 and 2021, we conducted 11 interviews with current and former U.S. intelligence leaders and policymakers whose careers spanned multiple administrations. We asked about (1) their direct experience with intelligence estimates, (2) bias in intelligence or policymaking, and (3) specific examples of internal or external bias that they might have witnessed or of which they were aware. Furthermore, we reviewed historical literature and analyses of suspected bias in or influence on intelligence processes, descriptions of intelligence "failures," memoirs of senior officials, and other literature to identify any instances of bias or influence that altered estimates or assessments. Finally, we analyzed the interviews and literature for themes related to trust or a lack thereof in the IC in general and of intelligence estimates in particular by U.S. policymakers, including the President.

Organization of the Report

In Chapter Two, we provide an overview and analysis of the literature. In Chapter Three, we examine some of the interactions between presidential administrations and the IC during the early Cold War (i.e., before 1980), focusing specifically on the administrations of John F. Kennedy, Lyndon B. Johnson, and Richard Nixon. In Chapter Four, we cover 1980 to the end of the Cold War, focusing on the Ronald Reagan administration's relationship with the IC and touching lightly on the administration of George H. W. Bush. In Chapter Five, we explore the administration of Bill Clinton and its interactions with the IC after the Cold War, highlighting changes in public trust in the IC. In Chapter Six, we explore the relationship between the administration of George W. Bush and the IC, with a specific focus on the events surrounding analysis that led to the war in Iraq. In Chapter Seven, we examine the administration of Barack Obama and its interactions with the IC. In particular, we discuss events surrounding the attack on the U.S. consulate in Benghazi, Libya, and the raid on Osama bin Laden's compound in Pakistan. In Chapter Eight, we provide an initial overview of the administration of Donald Trump and its relationship with the IC. We provide final thoughts, conclusions, and some recommendations for improving the relationship between policymakers and intelligence providers in Chapter Nine. Appendix A includes our decisionmaker interview protocol, and Appendix B details our IC member interview protocol. In Appendix C, we outline our literature search strategy and discuss limitations.

CHAPTER TWO

Literature Review

In an oft-cited work on the paradoxes of strategic intelligence, Woodrow Kuhns notes that "[t]he study of intelligence failures is perhaps the most academically advanced field in the study of intelligence."[1] In this study, we considered and expanded on this academically advanced field by focusing on two important factors of intelligence: bias and trust. Although bias and trust exist in intelligence even when there are no "intelligence failures," they are often part and parcel of the same conversation. Therefore, when we considered the extant literature, we found that much of it focuses on intelligence failures. After reviewing the literature, we found that it can be separated by level of analysis: individual, organizational, and interactional. Much of the early research focuses on the importance of individuals and psychology with regard to bias and trust in intelligence. Another important strain of the research emphasizes the role of bureaucratic processes and organizational factors. More-recent analyses examine the interactions between the IC and policymakers. Finally, there are several authors who split levels of analysis and attribute bias, trust, and failures to some combination of the three variables.

In the following sections, we discuss each level of analysis and highlight some important works that describe bias, trust, and intelligence failures in terms of those levels.

---

[1] Woodrow J. Kuhns, "Intelligence Failures: Forecasting and the Lessons of Epistemology," in Richard K. Betts and Thomas G. Mahnken, eds., *Paradoxes of Strategic Intelligence: Essays in Honor of Michael I. Handel,* London: Routledge, 2003, p. 80.

The Individual and Psychological Level

People are a key, common driver behind intelligence estimates and policy decisions.[2] This simple observation introduces a host of possible reasons for problems with bias and trust. People are liable to make mistakes, are susceptible to biases, and are not always rational in thought or action. Early work on deterrence theory highlighted how game theory was an imperfect way to wargame nuclear attacks because people do not always act rationally.[3] More importantly, motivated and unmotivated biases can color the way people think and act in everyday situations. Intelligence estimates are subject to the same types of psychological pressures. Michael Handel, in his book *War, Strategy, and Intelligence,* noted that "[t]he root of the problem—the weakest link in the intelligence process—is human nature."[4] The *9/11 Commission Report* highlights how psychological factors affected U.S. plans and actions in the lead-up to the September 11, 2001, terrorist attacks (9/11). The report notes that

> The most important failure was one of imagination. We do not believe leaders understood the gravity of the threat. The terrorist danger from Bin Ladin and al Qaeda was not a major topic for policy debate among the public, the media, or in the Congress.[5]

Moreover, the report notes, "Action officers should have been able to draw on all available knowledge about al Qaeda in the government. Management

---

[2] The use of artificial intelligence and machine learning has started to play a role in intelligence analysis, but it is important to recognize the possible bias introduced by algorithms and other elements of the computing process that were designed by people.

[3] For more information on psychology and deterrence, see Robert Jervis, Richard Ned Lebow, and Janice Gross Stein, *Psychology and Deterrence,* Baltimore, Md.: Johns Hopkins University Press, 1985.

[4] Michael I. Handel, *War, Strategy, and Intelligence,* New York: Frank Cass and Company, 1989, p. 34.

[5] National Commission on Terrorist Attacks Upon the United States, *The 9/11 Commission Report: Final Report of the National Commission on Terrorist Attacks Upon the United States—Executive Summary,* Washington, D.C., 2004b, p. 9.

should have ensured that information was shared and duties were clearly assigned across agencies, and across the foreign-domestic divide."[6]

9/11 is not the only event that scholars have ascribed to psychological attributes. Klaus Knorr discussed the Cuban Missile Crisis, criticizing congressional conclusions about why the Central Intelligence Agency (CIA) did not discover the missiles in Cuba more quickly. Knorr wrote that "[t]he most plausible explanation seems to me that this was a case of *apparent* 'behavioral surprise.' The [Soviet Union] adopted a course of action that *seemed* to be in conflict with our set of basic expectations about Soviet behavior, but actually was not." Knorr also noted that

> we may go wrong in an intelligence estimate, not because our operational set of expectations is faulty, but because we do not know the information (and perhaps the basic values) on which an opponent acts, or because we simply assume that he acts on approximately the same information (and basic values) which we have and that he will not make any technical mistakes in his calculations.[7]

Knorr argued that the IC was not able to more accurately assess what the Soviet Union would do because of assumptions that the analysts made when producing estimates.

Psychological pressures can influence both policymakers and the IC.[8] With regard to policymakers, Robert Jervis noted that

> [f]or reasons of both psychology and politics, decision makers want not only to minimize actual value trade-offs but to minimize their own perception of them. Leaders talk about how they make hard decisions all the time, but like the rest of us, they prefer easy ones and will try to convince themselves and others that a particular decision is in fact not so hard.[9]

---

[6] National Commission on Terrorist Attacks Upon the United States, 2004b, pp. 10–11.

[7] Klaus Knorr, "Failures in National Intelligence Estimates: The Case of the Cuban Missiles," *World Politics*, Vol. 16, No. 3, April 1964, p. 464.

[8] Robert Jervis, *Why Intelligence Fails: Lessons from the Iranian Revolution and the Iraq War*, Ithaca, N.Y.: Cornell University Press, 2010a.

[9] Jervis, 2010a, p. 160.

The IC complicates this desire for easy decisions by presenting a more complicated picture of the situation. According to Jervis, "[i]t is not that intelligence usually points to policies other than those the leaders prefer, but only that it is likely to give decision makers a more complex and contradictory view than fits with their political and psychological needs."[10] In his study, Jervis outlined the role played by psychology and politics in the U.S. inability to see the weakness of Shah Mohammad Reza Pahlavi's regime in 1970s Iran and the assessment that Iraq had weapons of mass destruction (WMD) in 2002 and 2003.

Although these works represent just a slice of the literature on individuals and psychology with regard to trust and bias in intelligence estimates, they clearly outline the role that such mechanisms have played and could play in the future. However, individual and psychological motivations are not the only explanation to be found in the literature on intelligence.

The Bureaucratic, Process, or Organizational Level

A second strain of literature focuses on the bureaucratic processes and organizational factors that can introduce bias and degrade trust in intelligence estimates. Although psychological and individual-level factors are clearly important, the literature on this second level of analysis recognizes that those individuals act within a broader framework. The structure of the IC and the processes through which intelligence estimates must go highlight the importance of examining these broader organizational-level factors that might influence analyses and policy. Consider, for example, Intelligence Community Directive 203, which emerged from the 2004 Intelligence Reform and Terrorism Prevention Act. The directive mandates specific analytic standards meant to reduce bias and politicization in IC analysis. The directive highlights the standards governing the "production and evaluation of analytic products" and outlines analytic standards by which all analysts must abide.[11] We examined the existing procedures and standards for

---

[10] Jervis, 2010a, p. 162.

[11] Intelligence Community Directive 203, *Analytic Standards*, Office of the Director of National Intelligence, January 2, 2015, p. 1.

insights into the process of intelligence analysis, but we recognize that even though there are community-wide process standards, individual agencies of the IC tend to focus on measuring and enforcing different aspects of the analytic standards and might be more or less restrictive in their application of standards. More importantly, the existence of such standards shows the extent to which estimates might be influenced by process or organizational elements.

These bureaucratic-level factors can influence both intelligence processes and products. Analyst Kristan Wheaton argued that intelligence products and intelligence processes need to be considered independently and that processes should receive the lion's share of attention. Wheaton wrote that

> the intelligence architecture, the system in which all the pieces are embedded, can be cumbersome, inflexible, and incapable of respond-ing to the intelligence needs of the decisionmaker. All are part of the intelligence process and any of these reasons—or any combination thereof—can be the cause of an intelligence failure.[12]

Wheaton also emphasized the importance of understanding the context and history of estimative judgments, writing that

> casting as broad a net as possible is important, to not only look at examples of where the intelligence product was false, but also cases where the intelligence product was true and, in turn, to examine the process in both cases to determine if the analysts were good or just lucky or bad or just unlucky.[13]

In this analysis, understanding the estimative process is clearly impor-tant for understanding where problems might arise. For our purposes, it is equally clear that the procedures may well affect trust in the IC.

Comparative work on intelligence has also yielded important insights into how the U.S. system creates an environment that is ripe for politici-zation. Uri Bar-Joseph and Philip H. J. Davies both found that the United

---

[12] Kristan J. Wheaton, "Evaluating Intelligence: Answering Questions Asked and Not," *International Journal of Intelligence and CounterIntelligence*, Vol. 22, No. 4, 2009, p. 621.

[13] Wheaton, 2009, p. 626.

States has unique structures and factors through which bias can be introduced.[14] Bar-Joseph noted that those factors are

1. the presidential system, which makes the President an independent political actor
2. intelligence products, which have become highly relevant to policy debates
3. the IC must work to gain the President's ear.[15]

Intelligence professionals have noted the influence of these structures as well. Richard Bissell, the CIA Deputy Director of Plans in the late 1950s and early 1960s, discussed the importance of the presidential system to intelligence. Bissell, who was fired after the failed Bay of Pigs invasion in Cuba, recalled a conversation he had with President Kennedy. While firing Bissell, Kennedy reportedly said, "If this were a parliamentary government, I would have to resign and you, a civil servant, would stay on. But being the system of government it is, a presidential government, you will have to resign."[16] Similarly, Philip Davies created a theory of *intelligence culture* to understand how parliamentary and presidential systems differ and how intelligence failures occur in each system. He analyzed his theory with an examination of the U.S. and UK governments and found that the systems in each contributed in unique ways to the estimates that Iraq had WMD.[17] With these works in mind, it is clear that analyzing the processes and organizations responsible for producing and consuming intelligence yields important insights into bias and trust in the IC.

---

[14] Uri Bar-Joseph, "The Politicization of Intelligence: A Comparative Study," *International Journal of Intelligence and CounterIntelligence*, Vol. 26, No. 2, 2013; Philip H. J. Davies, "Intelligence Culture and Intelligence Failure in Britain and the United States," *Cambridge Review of International Affairs*, Vol. 17, No. 3, 2004.

[15] Bar-Joseph, 2013, p. 361.

[16] Richard M. Bissell, Jr., *Reflections of a Cold Warrior: From Yalta to the Bay of Pigs*, New Haven, Conn.: Yale University Press, 1996, p. 191.

[17] Davies, 2004, p. 509.

The Interactional Level

Within the past ten years, several scholarly works have focused on the interactions between policymakers and the IC to see how politicization occurs.[18] These works focus on the potential disconnect between policy and intelligence. Intelligence has important limitations in what it can provide, but policymakers might not be cognizant of such constraints. These divisions could introduce important sources of bias (or degraded trust) in intelligence, as policymakers search for something that is not and cannot be there and intelligence officials see policymakers moving beyond the bounds of the analysis.

For example, Joshua Rovner analyzed several pathologies of IC-policymaker interactions. He noted that there are three categories of relations with potentially varying types within categories and varying types of relations. These categories are excessive harmony, in which "mutual satisfaction leads to shared tunnel vision;" neglect, in which the messenger is ignored or the IC self-isolates; and politicization.[19] According to Rovner, politicization can emerge from direct manipulation, indirect manipulation, embedded assumptions, intelligence subverting policy, intelligence parochialism, bureaucratic parochialism, partisan intelligence, and intelligence as a scapegoat.[20] More substantively, Rovner's analysis shows that we need to consider the ways in which policymakers are interacting with the IC to fully understand the sources of bias and trust.

---

[18] Beyond the scholarly literature, John Helgerson, Michael Morell, Bill Harlow, David Priess, and others provide first-hand accounts of what it is like to brief policymakers and how intelligence must adapt to be useful to the administration (John L. Helgerson, *Getting to Know the President, Second Edition: Intelligence Briefings of Presidential Candidates, 1952–2004*, Langley, Va.: Central Intelligence Agency, Center for the Study of Intelligence, 2012; Michael Morell and Bill Harlow, *The Great War of Our Time: The CIA's Fight Against Terrorism—from Al Qa'ida to ISIS*, New York: Grand Central Publishing, 2015; David Priess, *The President's Book of Secrets: The Untold Story of Intelligence Briefings to America's Presidents from Kennedy to Obama*, New York: Public Affairs, 2016).

[19] Joshua Rovner, *Fixing the Facts: National Security and the Politics of Intelligence*, Ithaca, N.Y.: Cornell University Press, 2011, p. 205.

[20] The table in Appendix A of Rovner (2011) contains the descriptions of these categories and types.

Mark Jensen also focused on the nature of the IC-policymaker interaction. He wrote that

> a major source of intelligence failures stems from a disconnect between what the IC can legitimately provide and what some decision-makers or vocal journalists expect. Contrary to what may be desired, omniscience about the past and present and clairvoyance about the future are not legitimate expectations of the IC.[21]

The insight that intelligence is limited in what it can provide is also noted in other works, including Betts (1978), who argues that intelligence failures are inevitable; Marrin (2011), who contends that 9/11 was a failure of policy and not strategic intelligence; and Pillar (2011), who looks at the challenges for the IC in presenting unwelcome messages.[22] Still other works argue that the IC cannot be omniscient or be solely responsible for policy failures.

Another potential scenario occurs when the IC has a finding but cannot convince policymakers of its import. In testimony before Congress in 2002, then–CIA director George Tenet discussed how the lack of actionable intelligence against al Qaeda hampered any policy actions against the terrorists prior to 9/11. Tenet said,

> Our collection sources 'lit up' during this tense period. They indicated that multiple spectacular attacks were planned, and that some of these plots were in the final stages. . . . But the reporting was maddeningly short on actionable details. The most ominous reporting, hinting at something large, was also the most vague.[23]

---

[21] Mark A. Jensen, "Intelligence Failures: What Are They Really and What Do We Do About Them?" *Intelligence and National Security*, Vol. 27, No. 2, 2012, p. 262.

[22] Richard K. Betts, "Analysis, War, and Decision: Why Intelligence Failures Are Inevitable," *World Politics*, Vol. 31, No. 1, October 1978; Stephen Marrin, "The 9/11 Terrorist Attacks: A Failure of Policy Not Strategic Intelligence Analysis," *Intelligence and National Security*, Vol. 26, Nos. 2-3, 2011; Paul R. Pillar, *Intelligence and U.S. Foreign Policy: Iraq, 9/11, and Misguided Reform*, New York: Columbia University Press, 2011.

[23] U.S. House and U.S. Senate Joint Intelligence Committee, "Written Statement for the Record of the Director of Central Intelligence Before the Joint Inquiry Committee," October 17, 2002, p. 19.

With these considerations in mind, we found that the IC-policymaker inter-action is important when assessing bias and trust. Policymakers might have unreasonable expectations about what the IC can provide, while the IC might fail to convince policymakers that there are suitable courses of action to take.

Split Levels of Intelligence Analysis

Some scholarly work has straddled the three levels of analysis discussed ear-lier. Scholars have attributed intelligence failures and politicization to some combination of psychological, organizational, or interactional variables. Each level contains important insights, and it is important to consider how each of the factors might interact and blend.

Bar-Joseph and Levy (2009) show one preeminent example of this split-level approach. The authors examined instances in which conscious, politically motivated behavior leads to intelligence failures. Specifically, they considered "intelligence to please, organizational restructuring, and insubordination."[24] They noted that "[a]lthough we have identified sev-eral analytically distinct sources of intelligence failure at different levels of analysis, we should emphasize that most intelligence failures are the prod-uct of the interaction of multiple factors at different levels."[25] Furthermore,

> In an unambiguous informational environment, psychological biases have a much weaker impact. . . . In an inherently ambiguous infor-mational environment, psychological biases and other variables play a much greater role. . . . Organizational cultures that are conducive to the free flow of information can be compromised by a key intelligence official who has an authoritarian management style and intolerance for dissent.[26]

---

[24] Uri Bar-Joseph and Jack S. Levy, "Conscious Action and Intelligence Failure," *Political Science Quarterly*, Vol. 124, No. 3, Fall 2009, p. 462.

[25] Bar-Joseph and Levy, 2009, p. 476.

[26] Bar-Joseph and Levy, 2009, p. 476.

Finally, they concluded, "[t]hese relationships are complex and context dependent, and as a result, there is no single path to intelligence failure, but instead multiple paths."[27]

Another scholarly work, Zegart (2005),

> attributes the adaptation failure of U.S. intelligence agencies to three factors: the nature of bureaucratic organizations, which makes internal reform exceedingly difficult; the self-interest of presidents, legislators, and government bureaucrats, which works against executive branch reform; and the fragmented structure of the federal government, which erects high barriers to legislative reform.[28]

Other scholarly works that split levels of analysis are Betts (2007), Gentry (2008), and Handel (1987).[29] These works shed light on the degree to which individuals operate within organizations that must interact with policymakers. Bias and trust (or the lack thereof) can play important roles in each step, and the literature that splits levels of analysis shows how each component influences the others.

Levels of Analysis over Time

Throughout this report, we discuss bias in intelligence across several different periods: the early Cold War (before 1981); the Reagan and George H. W. Bush administrations; and separately for the Clinton, George W. Bush, Obama, and Trump administrations. Organizing the analysis temporally revealed an important insight: The levels of analysis that we discussed earlier are present in varying degrees in each time frame. It is important to note

---

[27] Bar-Joseph and Levy, 2009, p. 476.

[28] Amy B. Zegart, "September 11 and the Adaptation Failure of U.S. Intelligence Agencies," *International Security*, Vol. 29, No. 4, Spring 2005, pp. 79–80.

[29] Richard K. Betts, "Two Faces of Intelligence Failure: September 11 and Iraq's Missing WMD," *Political Science Quarterly*, Vol. 122, No. 4, Winter 2007/2008; John A. Gentry, "Intelligence Failure Reframed," *Political Science Quarterly*, Vol. 123, No. 2, Summer 2008; Michael Handel, "The Politics of Intelligence," *Intelligence and National Security*, Vol. 2, No. 4, 1987.

that this report is not making an argument about which level of analysis is most appropriate for analyzing bias and trust in intelligence estimates; we simply mean to suggest that levels of analysis are a useful organizing principle and lens with which to view the relevant literature.

Our examination of the early Cold War period shows both individual- and organizational-level factors at work. During the Bay of Pigs invasion, President Kennedy made important changes to the plan (representing individual-level influence), while CIA officials became advocates for specific policy positions (representing organizational-level influence). Similarly, during the controversy over the order of battle in Vietnam, we found individual- and process-level elements. There are specific episodes in which administration officials sought to change analyses to better fit the policy line. The U.S. Department of Defense (DoD) and CIA also used different processes to examine intelligence, leading to a disjuncture in the estimates. President Nixon's relationship with the IC revealed the importance of psychological factors; he was deeply distrustful of the CIA. Even with the heavy emphasis on the individual, an analysis of President Nixon and the potential capabilities of the Soviet Union's SS-9 missile also revealed important bureaucratic-level facets that influenced the assessments, including conflicts over conclusions and methodology among DoD, the National Security Council (NSC), and the CIA.

Similarly, we found each level of analysis in the late Cold War period. Individual-level factors were present when Soviet hawks ran the intelligence apparatus once President Reagan appointed William Casey as Director of Central Intelligence (DCI). Furthermore, there were significant process changes once Robert Gates took over as head of analysis for the CIA. We also found individual- and organizational-level biases in the Defense Intelligence Agency (DIA) throughout the 1980s.

The differing levels of analysis are also apparent in the Clinton and George W. Bush administrations, when the CIA was trying to find its footing after the end of the Cold War. Government and public trust in intelligence fell, and bias emerged over the attribution of the USS *Cole* attack. Furthermore, in the lead-up to the invasion of Iraq in 2003, we found that administration officials repeatedly questioned the conclusions of the intelligence community, disseminated their own intelligence analyses, and made public statements that were not supported by intelligence. We also found evidence of retaliation against dissenters and the IC self-adjusting in the face of sustained pressure.

The Obama and Trump administrations were no different in terms of how bias emerged: Individual- and organizational-level factors, including the IC-policymaker relationship, continued to affect intelligence estimates. Under President Obama, we found external bias with the CIA's "enhanced interrogation" programs. Bias also influenced counterterrorism policy and green force analysis, particularly within the DIA. There is also evidence of bias in talking points related to the attacks in Benghazi, Libya, and in the selective declassification of documents related to the War on Terror and to Cuba.

We found evidence that perceived bias in intelligence was particularly pernicious during the Trump administration. Organizational factors allowed policymakers to assume positions of power within the IC. Structurally, IC officials had no incentives to dissent. Moreover, individual-level factors also inhibited dissent: IC analysts looked to avoid conflict with policymakers and avoid charges of being part of the "deep state." Finally, Trump administration officials worked to get just enough "truthiness" into talking points to avoid contradicting intelligence.

All told, from the establishment of the IC in 1947 to the present, bias has emerged as a result of many factors at different levels of analysis. Individuals looked to avoid conflict and please political masters. The structure of the IC has created bureaucratic, organizational, and process imperatives that lead to biased intelligence. Finally, the relationships between policymakers and the IC frequently have displayed the emergence of bias. The preponderance of evidence in support of each level suggests that academics, commentators, and other writers who favor a split-level approach are fundamentally able to leverage a more nuanced and complete explanation for the emergence of bias in intelligence and the politicization of intelligence.

Conclusion

After reviewing the literature on bias in the IC, we propose that the scholarly work can be separated into four categories according to level of analysis. These are the individual and psychological level, bureaucratic process and organizational level, interactional level, and works that split levels of analysis. A final point of emphasis relates to the dependent variable (i.e., perceived bias). The literature on bias in the IC tends to cluster around significant events, such as the bombing of Pearl Harbor; the ill-fated Bay of Pigs invasion, the mistakes prior to 9/11, the controversies over Iraq's WMD program, and others. This is understandable: Significant failures draw the headlines; politicians, academics, and pundits have access to a wider array of information; and failures raise questions about how to avoid future problems. However, the focus on salient events, particularly failures, introduces important limitations in how we consider bias in the IC.

Noted scholar Robert Jervis raised this very point in a 2018 roundtable discussion. According to Jervis,

> [f]or decades, political scientists have been taught that it is dangerous if not forbidden to search on the dependent variable.... Yet almost all studies of intelligence failures have looked only at the failures themselves, without making comparisons with successes. This was true even of scholars who not only knew about this problem, but had stressed it in their teaching.[30]

Any study of bias in intelligence needs to recognize that much more time and attention is spent when things go wrong as opposed to when things work as they should. Consider, for example, the number of column inches, hours of airtime, and amount of ink spent on potential IC reforms after 9/11. By comparison, how many intelligence successes readily spring to mind? Indeed, in a speech before the CIA in 1961, President Kennedy said, "It is not always easy. Your successes are unheralded—your failures are trumpeted."[31] Because the corpus on intelligence successes is relatively spare, many are forced to draw conclusions that are based on incomplete comparisons.[32] Moreover, Steve Chan highlighted the cognitive biases that are attached to

---

[30] Robert Jervis, "Introduction by Robert Jervis, Columbia University: Roundtable 10-15 on *Intelligence Success and Failure: The Human Factor*," H-Diplo, *International Security Studies Forum Roundtable*, Vol. 10, No. 15, June 4, 2018.

[31] Center for the Study of Intelligence, *"Our First Line of Defense": Presidential Reflections on US Intelligence*, Washington, D.C., 1996.

[32] Notable exceptions are Uri Bar-Joseph and Rose McDermott, *Intelligence Success and Failure: The Human Factor*, New York: Oxford University Press, 2017; and Erik J.

making post hoc judgments on historical cases.[33] Therefore, when we discuss how bias is introduced into intelligence, we need to be cognizant of the times when it is not. Although we predominantly focus on particularly instructive episodes, we also include references from policymakers and intelligence officials on how the process should work. From these instances, we look to make the more structured comparison—analyzing both instances in which intelligence was biased and instances when it was not.

Dahl, *Intelligence and Surprise Attack: Failure and Success from Pearl Harbor to 9/11 and Beyond*, Washington, D.C.: Georgetown University Press, 2013.

[33] Steve Chan, "The Intelligence of Stupidity: Understanding Failures in Strategic Warning," *American Political Science Review*, Vol. 73, No. 1, March 1979.

CHAPTER THREE

Early Cold War (Before 1981): The Kennedy, Johnson, and Nixon Administrations

As opposed to some European countries, which have centuries of expertise in gathering and disseminating intelligence, the United States is a relative newcomer to the intelligence game. In an oft-quoted phrase, former U.S. Secretary of State Henry L. Stimson said, "Gentlemen do not read each other's mail," as he closed the Black Chamber, the State Department's decryption unit, in 1929.[1] After the onset of World War II, U.S. deficiencies in intelligence were quickly made obvious, not least because of the surprise attack on Pearl Harbor.[2] President Franklin D. Roosevelt worked quickly to remedy these issues, empowering the Coordinator of Information—and, later, the Office of Strategic Services—to gather and analyze intelligence.[3] Although President Truman shut down the Office of Strategic Services after World War II, the need for a foreign intelligence–gathering service was once again

---

[1] Henry L. Stimson and McGeorge Bundy, *On Active Services in Peace and War*, New York: Hippocrene Books, 1971, p. 188.

[2] For a full account of the intelligence in the lead-up to Pearl Harbor, see Roberta Wohlstetter, *Pearl Harbor: Warning and Decision*, Stanford, Calif.: Stanford University Press, 1962.

[3] For a useful overview of the development of U.S. intelligence during World War II, see Patrick K. O'Donnell, *Operatives, Spies, and Saboteurs: The Unknown Story of the Men and Women of World War II's OSS*, New York: Citadel Press Books, 2004. O'Donnell conducted several interviews with former Office of Strategic Services civilians and officers and sheds a considerable degree of light on the early stages of intelligence in the United States.

made obvious by the onset of the Cold War. The National Security Act of 1947 drastically changed the makeup of the military and intelligence side of the government, establishing the CIA as the preeminent agency for collecting and analyzing intelligence gathered abroad. Concerns quickly emerged about bias in the evaluation of evidence—or in the politicization of intelligence, which itself might stem from biases in the way in which evidence is evaluated or presented. Moving forward, we discuss major instances in the early Cold War in which internal or external biases influenced intelligence estimates and outline how those incidents emerged.

Creeping Bias in the Planning for the Bay of Pigs Invasion

Although the CIA was an active player in U.S. foreign policy through the 1950s, especially as President Dwight D. Eisenhower deployed intelligence officers to Iran and Guatemala to ensure that those regimes were amenable to the U.S. government, one of the first major instances in which internal and external biases influenced intelligence estimates was in the Bay of Pigs invasion in 1961. In this case, we found three primary ways in which bias was introduced. Specifically, the change in administrations between Presidents Eisenhower and Kennedy resulted in differing expectations about the feasibility of the plan, President Kennedy made several alterations to the operational plan that drastically changed the likelihood of success, and the CIA moved from a position of providing advice to actively advocating for a particular course of action.

Planning for the overthrow of the government of Fidel Castro in Cuba started in January 1960, just 11 months before the presidential election. Eisenhower approved the CIA's plan for an invasion in March 1960.[4] Although President-elect Kennedy was briefed on the plan around Thanksgiving 1960, he did not start voicing concerns until assuming office. However, the transition introduced a series of problems with regard to the feasi-

---

[4] For a timeline of Bay of Pigs planning, see U.S. Department of State, Office of the Historian, "The Bay of Pigs Invasion and Its Aftermath, April 1961–October 1962," *Milestones in the History of U.S. Foreign Relations: 1961–1968*, undated.

bility of the plan. The CIA's then–Deputy Director for Plans, Richard Bissell, noted in his autobiography that Eisenhower

> asked "What are the feasible means of helping to mobilize a stronger invasion force so that a failure in the first effort would not wipe out the whole project?" Unfortunately, as the plans for an invasion continued, we lost sight of this question. Just a few days later, Eisenhower would not be in a position to request an answer.[5]

Furthermore, Bissell noted that Kennedy was not in a position to overhaul the plans: "Complicating matters further, Kennedy inherited certain policy decisions of the previous administration and was under pressure to carry them out. Cuba was destined to become his baptism by fire."[6] Future CIA director Richard Helms echoed the problems created by the change in presidential administrations:

> The Kennedy administration was very new to the game. . . . No matter how well qualified the individual members of a new administration may be—and President Kennedy took office with a very strong staff—the first few weeks before any incoming administration settles down are not the most propitious time to risk radical foreign policy undertakings.[7]

President Kennedy also instituted a series of new tactical demands on the plans, particularly with regard to the landing site and air cover, that drastically changed the likelihood of the operation's success. First, Kennedy demanded that the landing be moved away from Trinidad. Bissell wrote that Trinidad, "while representing the best hope, was deemed 'too noisy' by Kennedy, and although he was willing to move ahead generally, he could not support a plan that he felt exposed the role of the United States so openly."[8]

---

[5] Bissell, 1996, p. 162.

[6] Bissell, 1996, p. 163.

[7] Richard Helms, *A Look over My Shoulder: A Life in the Central Intelligence Agency*, New York: Random House, 2003, p. 179.

[8] Bissell, 1996, p. 169.

More importantly, however, Kennedy gave the CIA only four days to change the plan. Bissell noted that

> [i]t is hard to believe in retrospect that the president and his advisers felt the plans for a large-scale, complicated military operation that had been ongoing for more than a year could be reworked in four days and still offer a high likelihood of success. It is equally amazing that we in the agency agreed so readily.[9]

Helms agreed, writing that the "original and more feasible landing area [had] been vetoed by President Kennedy."[10]

President Kennedy further revised the operation by reducing the amount of air support before the invasion and canceling a second wave of bombers at the last minute. Bissell discussed how Kennedy "wanted to play down the magnitude of the invasion in the public eye and therefore did not want a full-strength strike but a more limited one."[11] Bissell responded by cutting the first strike in half, from 16 aircraft down to eight. Furthermore, on April 16, 1961, the President decided to cancel the second wave of strikes. Bissell wrote that "[t]he main effect of these successive decisions was that eight sorties were flown before the invasion took place instead of the hoped-for forty plus."[12] Helms argued that the canceled air strikes had a severe effect on the operation: "After President Kennedy refused to provide the desperately needed additional air support and their ammunition was almost exhausted, the men had no choice but to surrender."[13] While Bissell acknowledged that the CIA could have been more forceful in arguing for the original landing site and the necessity of air strikes, Kennedy biased the estimates by refusing to accept intelligence assessments. Bissell wrote that "Kennedy found

---

[9] Bissell, 1996, p. 169.

[10] Helms, 2003, p. 179.

[11] Bissell, 1996, p. 183.

[12] Bissell, 1996, p. 184.

[13] Helms, 2003, p. 179.

the new arrangement still too noisy. He asked repeatedly whether the air strikes were necessary; in effect, he wouldn't take yes for an answer."[14]

Finally, in addition to the external pressure from the Kennedy administration to change operational plans, the CIA displayed a sunk-cost bias and moved into a position of advocating for a particular policy option. Bissell, as Deputy Director for Plans, should have been in a position to provide objective analysis on the likelihood of success. Instead, he and the CIA advocated for the invasion approach. Bissell wrote that "the agency was so committed to the Cuban invasion plan and so sure of it at this juncture that [CIA director Allen] Dulles and I were edged into the role of advocates."[15] Bissell also noted that

> The physical impossibility of calling off the invasion, as well as the emotional toll that would entail, was an important factor in our actions. It could very well be that the fear of cancellation became so absorbing that I managed to ignore or suppress relevant facts. . . . It is also possible that we in the agency were not as frank with the president about further deficiencies as we could have been.[16]

The Bay of Pigs invasion was not, however, the only situation in the early Cold War period during which bias was introduced into the estimative process of intelligence.

Politicization over the North Vietnamese Order of Battle

In this section, we discuss how the Johnson administration pressured intelligence officials to "get on the team" with regard to the crossover point in Vietnam. By the mid-1960s, the Johnson administration had put together a public relations campaign to convince American voters that the U.S. military was making progress in its fight against Vietnamese communists. In

---

[14] Bissell, 1996, p. 170.

[15] Bissell, 1996, p. 172.

[16] Bissell, 1996, p. 173.

June 1967, the Office of National Estimates started drafting Special National Intelligence Estimate (SNIE) 14.3-67, which dealt with the capabilities of enemy forces in South Vietnam.[17] The perceived bias in the order-of-battle (O/B) estimates was the direct result of politicized intelligence by both the military and officials in the Johnson administration.

Joshua Rovner called the Johnson administration's attempts to sway CIA estimates on the O/B in Vietnam a "direct manipulation of intelligence to reflect policy preferences." Rovner noted that "[h]igh-level policymakers tried to influence the estimate so that it appeared to support the ongoing public relations effort."[18] The administration's attempt to bias the estimate was the result of a difference between U.S. Military Assistance Command, Vietnam (MACV) and the CIA in how to properly assess combatants. MACV did not include nonmilitary supporting groups, political officers, self-defense forces, or the Assault Youth in their estimates of guerrilla strength. In contrast, the CIA argued that all those groups should be included because of their contributions to the overall war effort. MACV refused to budge from its position that the count of enemy end strength totaled 298,000; the CIA estimated total forces to be around 491,000.

The CIA's estimate of the end strength of the enemy forces would have directly undercut the public relations campaign, and both the military and the administration worked to prevent just such an event. General Creighton Abrams, the deputy commander of MACV, said,

> If [Viet Cong self-defense forces] and [Viet Cong secret self-defense forces] are included in the overall enemy strength, the figure will total 420,000 to 431,000. . . . This is in sharp contrast to the current overall strength figure. . . . We have been projecting an image of success over the recent months. . . . Now, when we release [this] figure . . . the newsmen will . . . [draw] an erroneous and gloomy conclusion as to the meaning of the increase. . . . In our view the strength figures for the

---

[17] Special National Intelligence Estimate 14.3-67, *Capabilities of the Vietnamese Communists for Fighting in South Vietnam*, Washington, D.C.: Central Intelligence Agency, Office of National Estimates, November 13, 1967.

[18] Rovner, 2011, p. 73.

[self-defense forces] and [secret self-defense forces] should be omitted entirely from the enemy strength figures in the forthcoming [SNIE].[19]

The most prominent episode of bias being introduced into the estimative intelligence of the strength of the enemy occurred at a 1967 conference in Saigon with representatives of the military and CIA. At the meeting, George Carver, the CIA's special assistant for Vietnamese affairs, concluded that General William Westmoreland's staff had been ordered that the enemy strength count not exceed 300,000. Carver cabled headquarters, saying that "So far, our mission frustratingly unproductive since MACV stone-walling, obviously under orders . . . [My] inescapable conclusion [is] that [MACV] has given instruction tantamount to direct order that [Viet Cong] strength total will not exceed 300,000 ceiling." More importantly, Carver wrote in the telegram, "[r]ationale seems to be that any higher figure would generate unacceptable level of criticism from the press."[20] Harold Ford echoed this conclusion in a postmortem for the CIA:

> [T]he most important regulator of the MACV O/B estimates was the fact that General Westmoreland and his immediate staff were under a strong obligation to keep demonstrating 'progress' against the Communist forces in Vietnam. . . . [I]t would be politically disastrous, they felt, suddenly to admit . . . that the enemy's strength was in fact substantially greater than MACV's original or current estimates.[21]

Military representatives at the Saigon conference later acknowledged that they were operating under such an order. Colonel Gaines Hawkins, the chief of MACV's O/B section, told a CIA official that "[o]ur hands are tied; this is a command position; we have to stay within a total figure of 300,000; I personally share your 500,000 estimate, but we cannot accept it."[22]

---

[19] As quoted in Harold P. Ford, *CIA and the Vietnam Policymakers: Three Episodes 1962–1968*, Langley, Va.: Central Intelligence Agency, Center for the Study of Intelligence, 1998, p. 85.

[20] Quoted in Helms, 2003, p. 324.

[21] Ford, 1998, p. 87.

[22] Hawkins relayed this information to George Allen, a CIA military analyst; quoted in Ford, 1998, p. 91.

The military was not the only government body seeking to politicize the CIA's estimates on the O/B. Ambassador Robert Komer, chief of the Office of Civil Operations and Rural Support and a close friend of President Johnson, actively worked to change the estimates. George Allen, a veteran CIA military analyst, recounted a conversation that Komer had with Carver. Komer reportedly said, "You guys simply have to back off. Whatever the true O/B figure is, is beside the point. . . . [If] some dove in State will leak it to the press; that will create a public disaster and undo everything we've been trying to accomplish out here."[23] Allen was also the recipient of politicization from National Security Advisor Walt Rostow. Rostow reportedly once told Allen, "I'm sorry you won't support your president."[24]

At the end of the Saigon conference, Carver acceded to the military's demands: The CIA changed its estimates of the strength of the Vietnamese communists. CIA director Richard Helms later wrote,

> It is much to President Johnson's credit that never at any time did he request or suggest that I change or moderate any estimates or intelligence reports. . . . This could not have been said about the members of his staff who frequently challenged our work with infuriating suggestions that we "get on the team"—that is, trim our reporting to fit policy.[25]

The SNIE, which was published with the military's estimates, went to policymakers on November 13, 1967.

President Nixon's Suspicions About the Intelligence Community

Nixon came into office deeply suspicious of the CIA, believing that it was staffed with "northeastern liberals and detached intellectuals," and that it

---

[23] Quoted in Ford, 1998, p. 97.

[24] Quoted in Rovner, 2011, p. 73.

[25] Helms, 2003, p. 328.

had tainted the 1960 election with the myth of the missile gap.[26] Moreover, during his time in office, President Nixon said that the CIA was "disloyal," "unproductive," "over-staffed," and "not worth a damn;" at one point, he asked, "What the hell do those clowns do out there in Langley?"[27] Nixon also told confidants that he wanted CIA director Richard Helms barred from NSC meetings, while National Security Adviser Henry Kissinger tried to get Helms fired.

Amid this acrimonious relationship, Nixon administration officials sought to bias intelligence estimates to support administration policies. One particularly telling episode dealt with the assessments of the capabilities of the Soviet Union's new SS-9 intercontinental ballistic missile (ICBM) and of Soviet premier Leonid Brezhnev's intentions regarding the missile. President Nixon came into office with a strong emphasis on security. One of his first policy priorities was missile defense. Moving on from President Johnson's Sentinel program, Nixon championed Safeguard, a proposal in which Minuteman ICBMs would be paired with anti-ballistic missile (ABM) systems.[28] In making arguments for Safeguard, the Nixon administration politicized two highly relevant factors in support of the policy: first, that the missile had multiple independently targetable reentry vehicles (MIRVs), and second, that the Soviet Union sought first-strike capabilities. Administration officials, including the President, introduced this bias in several ways. First, the administration selectively declassified intelligence in support of its position. Additionally, in public statements, officials referred obliquely to the fact that still-classified intelligence provided more-concrete support. Second, the administration directly pressured the IC to remove dissent from estimates.

President Nixon and Secretary of Defense Melvin Laird both gave public statements referring to the intelligence in support of the need for the Safe-

---

[26] Rovner, 2011, pp. 89, 33. The *myth of the missile gap* was a notion that was prevalent among analysts in the United States that the Soviet Union was developing missiles more quickly and in larger quantities than the United States was.

[27] Christopher R. Moran and Richard J. Aldrich, "Trump and the CIA: Borrowing from Nixon's Playbook," *Foreign Affairs*, April 24, 2017.

[28] Lawrence Freedman, U.S. *Intelligence and the Soviet Strategic Threat*, Princeton, N.J.: Princeton University Press, 1977, p. 131.

guard system. Nixon, in a press conference on April 18, 1969, said, "I analyzed the nature of the threat. I found, for example, that even since the decision to deploy the ABM system called Sentinel in 1967, the intelligence estimates indicated that the Soviet capability with regard to their SS-9's, their nuclear missiles, was 60 percent higher than we thought then." He then doubled down on potential threats to the United States:

> The Chinese Communists, according to our intelligence, have not moved as fast recently as they had over the past 3 to 4 years, but that, nevertheless, by 1973 or 1974 they would have a significant nuclear capability which would make our diplomacy not credible in the Pacific unless we could protect our country against a Chinese attack aimed at our cities.[29]

On June 19, 1969, in another press conference, President Nixon said, "in recommending Safeguard, I did so based on intelligence information at that time. Since that time new intelligence information with regard to the Soviet success in testing multiple reentry vehicles—that kind of information, has convinced me that Safeguard is even more important."[30]

In congressional testimony, Laird made similar comments. In a hearing on intelligence and the ABM system, Laird said, "The urgency we attach to implementing the President's Safeguard proposal is based on our judgment as policymakers that the intelligence available up to this time clearly shows that the Soviet Union is constructing and deploying forces of a type and character inconsistent with mere deterrence."[31] Laird doubled down and asserted that the Soviets were manufacturing the SS-9 to achieve a first-strike capability: "I merely stated to this committee my belief that the Soviet Union was developing a first-strike capability. There was no question about

---

[29] Richard Nixon, "The President's News Conference," American Presidency Project, April 18, 1969a.

[30] Richard Nixon, "The President's News Conference," American Presidency Project, June 19, 1969b.

[31] U.S. Senate, *Intelligence and the ABM: Hearings Before the Committee on Foreign Relations*, Washington, D.C.: U.S. Government Printing Office, June 23, 1969, p. 6.

it in my mind, and I still believe that today."[32] The problem with Nixon's and Laird's statements, from the IC's point of view, was that nothing in the data actually suggested that the Soviet Union had the capability that the policy-makers asserted it did.

With regard to the CIA's view of the SS-9, director Richard Helms wrote in his memoir that "The Air Force, impressed by the SS-9's bulk, granted it an enormous capability [in throw weight]. Our experts thought it less powerful. The Pentagon military analysts considered the weapon to be highly accurate. The Agency team disagreed."[33] As for the Safeguard system, Helms wrote,

> If anything was likely to unleash the dollars needed to create an ABM, the specter of a score of SS-9's delivering sixty precisely guided missiles in one volley should have carried the day. Agency analysts disagreed, and remained convinced that any such independent guidance capability was beyond the grasp of Soviet science.[34]

According to Helms, Laird responded, saying, "Where . . . [does] CIA get off contradicting Nixon's policy?"[35] Also according to Helms, other senior members of the administration asked, "'Whose team is CIA on?' In other words, 'Let's all get together and trim the evidence to suit the wishes of the politicians.'"[36] Kissinger created a panel on the MIRV, which was chaired by the NSC, to "clarify the differences" between DoD and CIA.[37] A senior CIA official said that Kissinger warned, "Look . . . the president of the United States and the secretary of defense have said the following. Now, are you

---

[32] U.S. Senate, 1969, p. 7.

[33] Helms, 2003, p. 385.

[34] Helms, 2003, p. 385.

[35] Helms, 2003, p. 386.

[36] Helms, 2003, p. 387.

[37] Rovner, 2011, p. 100.

telling me that you're going to argue with them?"[38] Another NSC staffer said that the CIA analysis was "highly inconvenient" to the White House.[39]

The issue came to a head during the annual update of the national estimate of Soviet ICBM capability. CIA inserted a paragraph that "reaffirmed the earlier estimate—the [Soviet Union] was not seeking a first-strike capability. It also stated that the Soviets had not yet produced an SS-9 for testing, and expressed doubt that this could happen before 1974."[40] The CIA was quickly pressured to remove the paragraph. According to Joshua Rovner, DIA scientific advisory commission member Eugene Fabini "urged a colleague of Helms to persuade the DCI to delete the offending paragraph . . . [arguing] that it directly contradicted Laird's public statements."[41] Laird also "sent an assistant to ask Helms to remove the paragraph because it contradicted the public position of the Secretary."[42] Helms acceded to the administration's pressure:

> I was not prepared to stake the Agency's entire position on this one issue—in an average year CIA was making some sixty estimates, very few of which ever reached the President's level of concern. I was convinced we would have lost the argument with the Nixon administration, and that in the process the Agency would have been permanently damaged.[43]

Conclusion

Bias and intelligence estimates continued to be an issue throughout the rest of the Cold War. Rovner (2011) discusses the Ford administration and the Team B affair, while Jervis (2010) highlights the problems with intelligence related to the fall of the Shah of Iran in 1979. In terms of Team B, Rovner

---

[38] As quoted in Rovner, 2011, p. 100.

[39] As quoted in Rovner, 2011, p. 100.

[40] Helms, 2003, p. 386.

[41] Rovner, 2011, p. 102.

[42] Rovner, 2011, p. 102.

[43] Helms, 2003, p. 388.

notes that administration officials indirectly politicized estimates of the Soviet Union by allowing outspoken critics of détente to control the proceedings.[44] Meanwhile, Jervis argued that the CIA was unable to see the weakness in the Shah's regime because of "inadequate information, preexisting beliefs, mind sets, a small and isolated community of Iranian analysts, and a production system that emphasizes reporting events rather than underlying causes."[45]

Our discussion of the Bay of Pigs invasion, the estimates of the Vietnamese O/B, and the assessments of Soviet capabilities and intentions with regard to the SS-9 usefully illustrates the ways in which bias can be introduced and what the results of that bias can be. The Vietnamese O/B and SS-9 examples demonstrate the degree to which political officials will attempt to introduce bias in intelligence estimates to minimize any appearance of dissent. The Bay of Pigs example also highlights what happens when political officials make operational changes to plans without allowing the time to adequately consider the ramifications of such decisions. Overall, these instances show how the interactions between policymakers and intelligence providers can introduce a perceived bias into intelligence estimates. In the next chapter, we discuss bias and intelligence in the later Cold War.

---

[44] Rovner, 2011, pp. 114–116.

[45] Jervis, 2010a, p. 108.

CHAPTER FOUR

Late Cold War (1981–1993): The Administrations of Ronald Reagan and George H. W. Bush

Although the Kennedy through Ford administrations all had prominent episodes in which policymakers introduced bias, the Reagan and George H. W. Bush administrations had much less need to overtly influence intelligence assessments because one of their own was the director of the CIA. William Casey, the Office of Strategic Services veteran who famously mumbled his way through congressional testimony,[1] was the campaign manager for Reagan's 1980 presidential election. The former chairman of the Securities and Exchange Commission had revitalized Reagan's flagging campaign by rallying wealthy donors to the Republican cause. After Reagan's election, Casey expressed his desire to become Secretary of State. However, his unintelligible speech, his poor table manners, and Nancy Reagan's opposition meant that Casey would never become America's top diplomat.[2] Because of his wartime expertise and well-known hard-line credentials in terms of the Soviet Union, Reagan offered Casey the directorship of the CIA. The appointment itself revealed the Reagan administration's priorities. Uri Bar-Joseph discussed Casey's nomination as follows:

> [T]he 1981 nomination of William Casey as DCI in the Reagan administration was like nominating Team B to head the CIA. . . . [H]e was an

---

[1] Chris Whipple, *The Spymasters: How the CIA Directors Shape History and the Future*, New York: Scribner, 2020, p. 109.

[2] Whipple, 2020, p. 109.

ardent anti-Communist "cold warrior" and a key player in the administration's cultivation of the [Soviet Union] as "the evil empire"—a threatening force that stood behind each revolutionary movement in the Third World, every terrorist act in the Middle East, and plots like the assassination attempt on the Pope.[3]

Soviet Hawks in the Central Intelligence Agency

After the President appointed an established Soviet hawk—with cabinet rank and a direct line to the President—as DCI, IC officials started raising concerns about biased estimates. According to Joshua Rovner,

> [i]ntelligence analysts accused DCI William Casey, a charter member of the hawkish Committee on the Present Danger, of trying to turn the intelligence community into a propaganda mill for the administration. The mutual hostility that began during Cold War battles over the Soviet estimate never completely disappeared.[4]

Analysts, sensing the direction of the policy winds (and, in no small measure, attempting to please their direct supervisors), started to adopt a more hard-line stance against the Soviet Union. In this way, biased estimates emerged not from direct influence from policymakers or from the seventh floor of the CIA, but from analysts. In an analysis of the President's Daily Brief (PDB), the premier product of the IC, David Priess discussed how Casey's political leanings filtered down through the ranks:

> Casey's biggest impact on the PDB was indirect, via impressions that he would "politicize" assessments, or override experts' views to put them more in line with what policy makers wanted to see. Many analysts felt that Casey pushed his preferred conclusions on them, rather than letting them base their conclusions on an unbiased assessment of the facts on the ground.[5]

---

[3] Bar-Joseph, 2013, p. 351.

[4] Rovner, 2011, pp. 196–197.

[5] Priess, 2016, p. 143.

Other reports confirmed Casey's influence on CIA assessments. In a later evaluation of CIA directors, journalist and author Chris Whipple wrote, "Under Casey, the CIA would be totally dedicated to Reagan's agenda."[6] Whipple continued,

> In Casey's view . . . the agency's analysts had become intellectually flabby, academic, and cautious. 'This is a bunch of crap,' Casey would often write on papers he considered boring, badly written, or unimaginative. He was intellectually voracious, relentlessly seeking an edge over the Soviets, no matter how esoteric or dubious the source.[7]

In an anecdote about these predilections in practice, Whipple cited Casey's belief that the Soviet Union was controlling terrorists around the world, a view that was confirmed by Claire Sterling's book *The Terror Network: The Secret War of International Terrorism*. Sterling argued that the Soviets were controlling terrorist organizations; specifically, the Red Brigades in Italy, the Baader-Meinhof gang in Germany, and the Irish Republican Army.[8] After asking CIA analysts to confirm Sterling's finding—and incensed when the agency's experts disagreed—Casey reportedly said, "I paid $13.95 for this book, and it told me more than you bastards whom I pay $50,000 a year!"[9]

Pulitzer Prize–winning reporter and author Tim Weiner echoed many of the conclusions about Casey's influence over intelligence assessments at the CIA: "When Casey disagreed with his analysts, as he often did, he rewrote their conclusions to reflect his views. When he told the President, 'This is what the CIA thinks,' he meant, 'This is what I think.'"[10] Weiner cited comments from long-standing CIA analyst Dick Lehman, who said, "Working for Casey was a trial for everybody, partly because of his growing erraticism

---

[6] Whipple, 2020, p. 113.

[7] Whipple, 2020, p. 113.

[8] Claire Sterling, *The Terror Network: The Secret War of International Terrorism*, New York: Henry Colt and Company, 1981.

[9] Whipple, 2020, p. 114.

[10] Tim Weiner, *Legacy of Ashes: The History of the CIA*, New York: Doubleday, 2007, pp. 438–439.

and partly because of his own right-wing tendencies. . . . He was amenable to argument, but it took a hell of a lot of argument."[11] According to Weiner, Secretary of State George Schultz reportedly said, "The CIA's intelligence was in many cases simply Bill Casey's ideology."[12]

Changes to the Directorate of Intelligence Under Robert Gates

Although DCI William Casey was one of the most prominent voices pushing for harsher analyses of the Soviet Union, he was not alone in creating biased estimates. In 1982, Casey appointed Robert Gates, the future CIA director and Secretary of Defense, to be the Deputy Director for Intelligence (DDI), the chief of intelligence analysis and assessments. Gates instituted several changes in the analytical process that led many to accuse him of politicizing intelligence. These changes included a statement that senior CIA officers were now the most important consumers of intelligence, the establishment of quality as a key performance evaluator, a requirement that Gates would "review all [Directorate of Intelligence] products going to middle- or high-ranking consumers," and a rule that any divergent voices needed to be sent through office directors.[13] In practice, these changes might have allowed for the introduction of biased intelligence.[14] Former CIA intelligence analyst John A. Gentry wrote about the effect of Gates' new rules: "An internal CIA variant of Kremlinology thus arose, with office directors trying to figure out what Gates wanted, and subordinate managers and analysts trying to discern not only what Gates wanted, but what each of their superiors thought their bosses thought the DDI wanted."[15] Gentry quoted Directorate of Intelligence manager John Hibbits, who said,

---

[11] Weiner, 2007, p. 379.

[12] Weiner, 2007, p. 379.

[13] John A. Gentry, "Intelligence Analyst/Manager Relations at the CIA," *Intelligence and National Security*, Vol. 10, No. 4, 1995, p. 134.

[14] Gentry, 1995, p. 136.

[15] Gentry, 1995, p. 136.

How well agency managers could craft intelligence that would keep criticism from the DDI to a minimum became a measure of one's value and there arose a danger of being out of the loop if you were not responsive. Many professionals adjusted without seriously compromising the essential integrity of the product in their own mind, but it became difficult to remain completely objective.[16]

Uri Bar-Joseph discussed the degree to which Gates was perceived to influence intelligence assessments: "Under Gates the Intelligence Directorate started producing selective intelligence estimates that reflected the administration's political preferences, not only with regard to the magnitude of the Soviet threat, but also other global issues, from Iran's internal politics to the likelihood of a popular revolution in Mexico."[17]

Gates' influence as DDI struck some analysts as a direct manipulation of intelligence, creating bias in estimates. Melvin Goodman, a 24-year CIA veteran, even testified against Gates during his 1991 nomination for DCI. According to Goodman,

The issue was politicization for me—that is, the way that Bob Gates was taking intelligence and spinning it towards a policy purpose. My direct experience was on matters dealing with the Soviet Union and particularly the papal plot assessment of 1985, but actually intelligence was being politicized on a variety of issues dealing with Iran, Central America, Afghanistan, and the Middle East.[18]

Whipple also discussed the combined influence of Casey and Gates in relation to the analysis on the attempted assassination of the Pope. According to Whipple, "Casey insisted that the Soviets must be involved. He rejected initial reports on the episode, demanding evidence of Russian complicity. . . . Gates . . . made sure Casey got the answer he was looking for."[19] Whipple quoted an Italy-based operative as follows: "Gates wrote at

---

[16] As quoted in Gentry, 1995, p. 136.

[17] Bar-Joseph, 2013, p. 351.

[18] As quoted in Daniel Schulman, "CIA Veteran: How Robert Gates Cooked the Intelligence," *Mother Jones*, December 4, 2006.

[19] Whipple, 2020, p. 115.

the bottom of one of the papers that the Soviets were behind it, which corresponded with Casey's view. It's something that I would never do because we didn't have the evidence."[20] According to Whipple, Gates said that "[t]he paper basically said you couldn't prove [the Soviets] did it. . . . But because it adduced all the evidence we had that they did, some of the analysts who were involved were pissed off."[21]

Casey and Gates together ensured that the White House was seeing intelligence that confirmed the view of the Soviet Union as a dire threat. Goodman said that "Reagan wanted the highest defense increases in peacetime, and he needed an enemy to do that. . . . The exaggeration of the Soviet threat is what the White House called for—and that is what Casey and Gates worked so hard to give the president."[22]

The CIA was not the only member of the IC that was producing biased estimates through the late stages of the Cold War. In an interview with RAND researchers, a former intelligence official with DIA discussed biased intelligence during the Reagan and H. W. Bush years. The interviewee said that

> In DIA, there was significant politicization and bias in the production of analysis on Soviet and European topics. All products leaving the Agency were coordinated with the Defense Intelligence Officers (DIO), who worked directly for the Director. Analysts were well aware of the views of the officers and crafted papers and studies that would not draw a non-concurrence.[23]

Clearly, problems of perceived bias, particularly regarding the threat posed by the Soviet Union, were not restricted to the CIA.

---

[20] As quoted in Whipple, 2020, p. 115.

[21] Whipple, 2020, p. 115.

[22] As quoted in Whipple, 2020, p. 115.

[23] Former senior IC leader, interview with the authors.

Conclusion

What makes the intelligence estimates of the late Cold War unique is the source of the bias. In the early Cold War, and during the George W. Bush and Trump administrations, policymakers were the most frequent sources of politicized intelligence. Administration officials looking for intelligence to fit the policy line would pressure IC officials to deliver biased reports. However, during the late Cold War period, bias was predominantly introduced by IC officials who had distinct policy agendas themselves. DCI William Casey, a prominent Soviet hawk, exerted a high degree of influence over intelligence assessments. DDI Robert Gates made several changes within his directorate, making it easier for managers and other high-level officials to influence the content of analyses.

A natural question follows: How did the biased estimates influence tangible actions? Although biased estimates in the early Cold War period led to bungled covert operations and the extension of a war that was going poorly, the assessments through the 1980s resulted in one of the more significant intelligence misses in U.S. history: the failure to see or report on the collapse of the Soviet Union. The Reagan administration, along with DCI Casey and DDI Gates, favored assessments that portrayed the Soviet Union as a dire threat. Using these assessments, Reagan was able to pursue significant increases in defense spending. However, in truth, the Soviet Union was diminishing in power. Intelligence analysts either missed the fundamental weaknesses of the Soviet system or were not able to publish such estimates because they would not be accepted by senior leaders. For this reason, the IC did not adequately warn of an impending Soviet collapse. The inability to predict such an important event led to the gutting of the IC and introduced a host of new problems for an IC in search of a new enemy. We discuss these events in the next chapter.

CHAPTER FIVE

The Clinton Administration (1993–2001)

The Clinton administration was a pivotal time in the IC's history. When the Cold War ended, the IC's mission, and particularly that of the CIA, became muddied, and it was unclear where the IC fit into the U.S. national security apparatus.[1] The shift out of the Cold War proved difficult, particularly because an entrenched bureaucracy and risk-averse workforce impeded necessary organizational change in the transition away from a strict counter–Soviet Union focus.[2]

Despite this, the Clinton administration is not particularly known for any large-scale instances of biased intelligence—as one former policymaker noted in an interview with RAND researchers, there were some errors made under the Clinton administration, "but nothing major."[3] This is, in part, because President Clinton and his administration were motivated primarily by domestic political considerations. Any missteps might have been attributable (at least in part) to Clinton's lack of a strong relationship with the IC.

In this chapter, we expound on these events and the Clinton administration's policy calculus as it relates to the IC and intelligence at the time. In this chapter, we describe how Clinton's focus on domestic politics affected the extent to which he engaged with intelligence and what the repercus-

---

[1] James Risen, "The Nation; The Clinton Administration's See-No-Evil C.I.A.," *New York Times*, September 10, 2000.

[2] Risen, 2000; Christopher M. Jones, "The CIA Under Clinton: Continuity and Change," *International Journal of Intelligence and CounterIntelligence*, Vol. 14, No. 4, 2001, p. 505.

[3] Former policymaker, interview with the authors.

sions of his distant relationship with the IC were. We discuss the minimal relationship between President Clinton and the IC, the administration's focus on domestic politics, the impact of Aldrich Ames's arrest on espionage charges, and the claims of biased intelligence estimates with regard to the attack on the USS *Cole*.

The Intelligence Community's Role in the Absence of the Cold War

The President's relationship with and perceptions of the IC undoubtedly color the administration's decisionmaking and the importance it places on incoming intelligence analysis. President Clinton centered his presidency on domestic issues, which was a shift from his predecessors' foreign policy focus during the Cold War.[4] In an interview with the project team, one former intelligence official noted that "the change from Bush to Clinton was a seismic event."[5] The interviewee noted the contrast in prior experience between Clinton and George H. W. Bush, stating that "it was almost inevitable there would be a great collapse because Bush was so deeply woven into the IC and Clinton wasn't."[6] Clinton, who was concerned primarily with domestic issues, promised to focus "like a laser beam on the economy," reflecting the economic fallout of the contest with the Soviet Union.[7] The call for a "peace dividend," coupled with Clinton's emphasis on domestic issues, directly affected the IC budget and its relationship with the administration. Clinton reportedly cut the CIA's budgets by more than 25 percent.[8]

---

[4] Gentry, 2008, p. 256.

[5] Former intelligence official, interview with the authors.

[6] Former intelligence official, interview with the authors.

[7] As quoted in Steven Mufson, "Clinton to Send Message with Economic Choices," *Washington Post*, November 8, 1992; and Russell L. Riley, "Bill Clinton: Domestic Affairs," University of Virginia Miller Center, webpage, undated.

[8] Stansfield Turner, *Burn Before Reading: Presidents, CIA Directors, and Secret Intelligence*, New York: Hyperion Books, 2006, pp. 225–226, 235; Ron Suskind, *The One Percent Doctrine: Deep Inside America's Pursuit of Its Enemies Since 9/11*, New York: Simon and Schuster, 2006, p. 20; also cited in Gentry, 2008, p. 258.

Clinton was so distant from the IC that, in 1994, when a small plane landed on the White House lawn, it set off jokes that it was Clinton's first DCI, James Woolsey, trying to get a meeting with the President.[9] Louis Freeh, the director of the Federal Bureau of Investigation (FBI) during Clinton's tenure, had a similar experience, remarking that he met with Clinton one to three times over seven years.[10] Freeh writes that Clinton "just wasn't very interested in intelligence gathering or law enforcement."[11] In an interview with the research team, one former intelligence official noted that "a lot of people in the Clinton administration didn't understand the intel structure," and that "when [individuals] are not familiar with methods, and people are telling [them] these things as if they're facts, that can create some cognitive dissonance because [these] individuals are not accustomed to hearing this information from people who sound like they know what they're talking about."[12] This underscores the relative lack of understanding of the IC structure and intelligence tradecraft that colored the administration's relationship with the IC. This perhaps inhibited the administration's ability to engage with the IC and understand the analyses it provided.

In an oral history reflecting on his tenure as DCI, Woolsey noted that, specifically during the first two years, "intelligence [was] kind of on the back burner."[13] Woolsey also noted that he and the CIA briefer would effectively hand over the PDB to someone and they were rarely invited into the room, despite their desire to brief the President.[14] This estranged relationship was not unique to DCI Woolsey. Richard Haver, the former Director for Intelligence Community Affairs, recalls asking former DCI George Tenet how often he met with Bill Cohen, the Secretary of Defense in the latter

---

[9] Gentry, 2008, p. 256.

[10] Louis J. Freeh, *My FBI: Bringing Down the Mafia, Investigating Bill Clinton, and Fighting the War on Terror*, New York: St. Martin's Press, 2005, p. 246.

[11] Freeh, 2005, p. 246.

[12] Former intelligence official, interview with the authors.

[13] Robert James Woolsey, interview, Charlottesville, Va.: University of Virginia, Miller Center, William J. Clinton Presidential History Project, January 13, 2010, pp. 4–5.

[14] Robert James Woolsey, 2010, p. 18.

years of the Clinton administration. Tenet replied, "Never. I've never had a one-on-one meeting with Bill Cohen."[15]

It was not just President Clinton or individuals internal to the administration who placed less importance on the IC in the absence of the Cold War. There was also public-facing chatter questioning the CIA's utility. In a well-known 1991 opinion article, Senator Daniel Patrick Moynihan called for the dissolution of the CIA, suggesting that the Department of State could take over its responsibilities.[16] Although some sources indicate that Moynihan had previous grievances against the CIA, potentially motivating the op-ed, Moynihan's article is reflective of the post–Cold War mentality regarding the IC.[17] After describing a series of misjudgments on the part of the CIA regarding the Soviet economy, Moynihan went as far as stating that the CIA's post–Cold War activity would be nothing more than "a kind of retirement program for a cadre of cold warriors not really needed any longer."[18] Relatedly, the IC faced a shakeup in not only its mission but also its workforce. The post–Cold War era of analysts would need different skill sets as the threats to the United States changed, introducing the need for new priority languages and skills.[19] As one policymaker noted in an interview, there was a "reshuffling of IC analytical expertise after the Cold War" and there was increasing "recruitment of younger, new analysts right out of graduate school."[20] In the aforementioned interview with Woolsey, Haver noted that, while some elements of the community could pivot rather quickly, developing and crafting the human element would take considerably longer.[21]

---

[15] As quoted in Robert James Woolsey, 2010, pp. 20–21.

[16] Daniel P. Moynihan, "Opinion: Do We Still Need the C.I.A.? The State Dept. Can Do the Job," *New York Times*, May 19, 1991.

[17] Paul McGarr, "'Do We Still Need the CIA?' Daniel Patrick Moynihan, the Central Intelligence Agency and U.S. Foreign Policy," *History*, Vol. 100, No. 2, April 2015.

[18] Moynihan, 1991.

[19] Robert James Woolsey, 2010, pp. 72–73.

[20] Former policymaker, interview with the authors.

[21] Robert James Woolsey, 2010, p. 73.

Public Trust in Flux: The Ames Scandal

The need to reorganize the IC workforce was not only a result of the change in mission priorities. In 1994, it was revealed that Aldrich Ames, a veteran CIA officer, had been spying for Russia since 1985.[22] The Senate Select Committee on Intelligence started investigating Ames' activities after the criminal investigation was complete. The news that there had been a mole in the CIA for almost ten years was damaging enough, but perhaps the missed red flags in Ames's behavior were worse. For instance, the Committee report notes that, through money he received from the Russians, he was able to purchase a Jaguar and a $540,000 home on a salary of less than $70,000. These purchases did not alarm his colleagues.[23] In addition to sudden wealth, Ames had problems with alcohol abuse and series of security infractions.[24] The Ames scandal undoubtedly contributed to overall waning public trust in the IC in the post–Cold War environment. As the Committee report notes, the Ames incident revealed a profound "failure of the system."[25] The report also notes that the CIA could not withstand another similar event, citing concerns regarding public confidence.[26]

In 2001, the FBI experienced a similar scandal when a veteran FBI counterintelligence agent, Robert Hanssen, was arrested and charged with spying for Russia.[27] In the wake of the Ames scandal, running counter to the CIA Inspector General's (IG's) recommendation, director Woolsey sent letters of reprimand to only 11 employees (the CIA IG recommended reprimanding 23 employees) and did not suspend or demote—let alone fire—any employees.[28] The committee report notes that "[m]anagement accountabil-

---

[22] FBI, "History: Famous Cases and Criminals—Aldrich Ames," webpage, undated a.

[23] U.S. Senate Select Committee on Intelligence, *An Assessment of the Aldrich H. Ames Espionage Case and Its Implications for U.S. Intelligence*, Washington, D.C.: U.S. Government Printing Office, November 1, 1994, p. 1.

[24] U.S. Senate Select Committee on Intelligence, 1994, pp. 8–9.

[25] U.S. Senate Select Committee on Intelligence, 1994, p. 53.

[26] U.S. Senate Select Committee on Intelligence, 1994, p. 53.

[27] FBI, "History: Famous Cases and Criminals—Robert Hanssen," webpage, undated b.

[28] U.S. Senate Select Committee on Intelligence, 1994, p. 54.

ity within the Intelligence Community should be no less than the highest levels found elsewhere in the Executive branch. Director Woolsey's actions do not meet this standard."[29] By acting counter to the Committee's desires, Woolsey further entrenched public doubts about the IC at the time.

(Non)Attribution of the USS *Cole* Bombing

Many journalists, academics, pundits, and politicians have discussed the IC, al Qaeda, and the missed opportunities in the lead-up to 9/11. In this section, we focus on the Clinton administration's counterterrorism efforts, specifically in the case of the USS *Cole* bombing, and particularly the issue of attribution and whether bias in the intelligence process played a role in the attribution of the attack. Al Qaeda emerged as a player well ahead of 9/11. Indeed, the terror group was responsible for bombings in Yemen; the 1993 World Trade Center bombing; and the embassy attacks in Nairobi, Kenya, and Dar es Salaam, Tanzania. Furthermore, the IC started warning of attacks on American soil in the 1990s.

The USS *Cole* bombing occurred on October 12, 2000, about a month before the presidential election and exactly five days before the final presidential debate.[30] Some scholars believe that, given the looming election, the Clinton administration did not want to attribute the attack and subsequently be expected to take action. For instance, according to Whipple,

> Neither the CIA nor the FBI would officially link the bombing [of the USS *Cole*] to Al Qaeda. According to one senior intelligence official, the agency deliberately repressed the intelligence. "We were told we could not assign the blame for the USS Cole attack to bin Laden because if we did that then the Clinton administration would have been forced to take action," he said. The message was "you cannot write about it, do not assign blame." A definitive finding, this official said, might have

---

[29] U.S. Senate Select Committee on Intelligence, 1994, p. 55.

[30] FBI, "History: Famous Cases and Criminals—USS Cole Bombing," webpage, undated c; Pete Erickson, Seth Loertscher, David C. Lane, and Paul Erickson, "Twenty Years After the USS Cole Attack: The Search for Justice," *Combating Terrorism Center Sentinel*, Vol. 13, No. 10, October 2020.

affected the upcoming presidential election. "The political commissars all thought that Gore would win, but it would have been a bad thing—Democrats would have been seen as weak—if we assigned blame to bin Laden and didn't do anything. And so nothing was ever done about the USS Cole."[31]

Additionally, one official stated that there was sufficient evidence to attribute the attack. In an interview with NBC News, chief of the U.S. Navy investigative task force, Mark Fallon said, "Within two weeks we had significant information [that] we felt . . . was solid evidence that the attack was linked not only to al-Qaida but to Osama bin Laden."[32]

However, we found limited evidence that bias in the estimative process played a central role in the (non)attribution of the USS *Cole* attack. For instance, one source notes that, in the pre-9/11 era, there was confusion regarding who was responsible for responding to terrorism and how terrorism fit into the conventional idea of war.[33] Erickson and colleagues cite Michael Sheehan, who was then Ambassador-at-Large for Counterterrorism at the Department of State, who said that some in the government viewed terrorism as "the cost of doing business in a dangerous world."[34] Sheehan's frustration with the lack of military action following the USS *Cole* bombing is best encapsulated by the following quote included in Richard Clarke's memoir. Sheehan reportedly said, "What's it going to take, [Richard Clarke]? . . . Does al Qaeda have to attack the Pentagon to get their attention?"[35] Furthermore, Tenet wrote that the intelligence did not suffice to conclude that bin Laden "and his leadership had had authority, direction,

---

[31] Whipple, 2020, p. 183.

[32] Michael Isikoff, "U.S. Failure to Retaliate for USS Cole Attack Rankled Then—and Now," NBC News, October 12, 2010.

[33] Erickson et al., 2020.

[34] Michael A. Sheehan, *Crush the Cell: How to Defeat Terrorism Without Terrorizing Ourselves*, New York: Three Rivers Press, 2008, quoted in Erickson et al., 2020, p. 47.

[35] Richard A. Clarke, *Against All Enemies: Inside America's War on Terror*, New York: Free Press, 2004, quoted in Erickson et al., 2020, p. 47.

and control over the attack," and he subsequently suggested that policy-makers should determine the standard of proof for military action.[36]

As we have attempted to relay, whether bias impeded attribution of the USS *Cole* bombing is not a binary answer. Some accounts suggest that the IC's assessments were intercepted by the administration's political motives surrounding the upcoming national election, while others indicate a general lack of concern regarding terrorism, which might have been the reason for a lack of attribution.

Conclusion

As we discussed in this chapter, the Clinton administration represented an inflection point in U.S. history and the IC's history. Following the Cold War, the IC struggled to reorient its mission, while the incoming Clinton administration shifted its priorities away from foreign policy to domestic issues. As we have attempted to convey, the administration's domestic focus contributed to its particularly weak relationship with the IC. Clinton himself maintained a distant relationship with the IC, seldom meeting with his DCI and FBI directors. The fractured relationship between the IC and the administration had consequences, from management of the Aldrich Ames revelations to the lack of attribution of the USS *Cole* bombing. In the following chapter, we discuss the impact of 9/11 on the IC and how bias played into the Global War on Terror.

---

[36] George Tenet and Bill Harlow, *At the Center of the Storm: My Years at the CIA*, New York: HarperCollins Publishers, 2007, p. 128.

CHAPTER SIX

The George W. Bush Administration (2001–2009)

The 1990s brought many changes to the IC. Without the lingering threat of the Soviet Union, many experienced personnel retired or were forced out. There were even calls to completely abolish the CIA because of its performance at the end of the Cold War.[1] However, the attacks on 9/11 and the War on Terror meant that the IC became more important than ever in confronting new threats. Despite this vital mission, biased intelligence estimates continued to be a problem. George W. Bush administration officials pressured the IC for specific findings, and the IC made adjustments to stay relevant at the expense of analytical soundness. Interviews with policymakers and IC officials revealed biases over multiple issues, including the 9/11 attacks, the Iraq War, European support for U.S. involvement in the Middle East, the Olympics in Greece, Latin America and Venezuela's Hugo Chavez, and the troop surge in Afghanistan. In this chapter, we focus on the Bush administration's use of intelligence in advance of the invasion of Iraq in March 2003.

The administration pressured and politicized two interconnected—but distinct—issues. First was Iraqi leader Saddam Hussein's pursuit and purported possession of WMD.[2] Second were the links between the Iraqi regime

---

[1] Moynihan, 1991.

[2] One important consideration with regard to the IC's handling of information on Iraq's WMD is from the Silberman and Robb Commission report, commonly known as the WMD Commission report. Silberman and Robb note that "[a]fter a thorough review, the Commission found no indication that the Intelligence Community distorted the evidence regarding Iraq's weapons of mass destruction. What the intelligence

and al Qaeda, the organization responsible for the 9/11 attacks. Administration officials had one clear goal in biasing the intelligence: to sell the war to the American public.[3] Tellingly, former IC officials, including the DCI George Tenet and the National Intelligence Council's Paul Pillar, and academics argued that the Iraq War would have happened regardless of what the intelligence said. Pillar, in particular, highlighted how neoconservatives had been pushing for regime change in Iraq since Operation Desert Storm. This conclusion was echoed by Patrick Conway, who argues that the neoconservatives in the Bush administration were bent on war regardless of IC conclusions about WMD or links to al Qaeda.[4] Joshua Rovner similarly highlights how biased intelligence became relevant in the march to Iraq only in the face of downward polling data.[5]

In the administration's efforts to garner public support for the Iraq War, biased intelligence emerged in several ways: repeated questioning by administration officials; the dissemination of questionable intelligence analyses by policy officials; administration officials giving public statements that were not supported by intelligence; IC officials facing repercussions after providing dissenting analyses; and the IC making self-adjustments to the estimates to stay relevant. In this chapter, we discuss each of these factors and outline how the bias emerged.

Repeated Questioning of Intelligence by Administration Officials

One of the hallmarks of the Bush administration's approach to the IC was repeated questioning over single issues. Rovner noted that the repeated

---

professionals told you about Saddam Hussein's programs was what they believed. They were simply wrong" (Laurence H. Silberman and Charles S. Robb, *The Commission on the Intelligence Capabilities of the United States Regarding Weapons of Mass Destruction: Report to the President of the United States*, Washington, D.C., March 31, 2005).

[3] Pillar, 2011; Rovner, 2011.

[4] Patrick Conway, "Red Team: How the Neoconservatives Helped Cause the Iraq Intelligence Failure," *Intelligence and National Security*, Vol. 27, No. 4, August 2012.

[5] Rovner, 2011.

questioning "led some analysts to suspect that policymakers were fishing for answers that reflected their own beliefs."[6] Former analysts also have discussed the effect of repeated questioning on the intelligence analysis process, including CIA official and counterterrorism expert Vincent Cannistraro, who said,

> The analysts are human, and some of them are also ambitious. What you have to worry about is the "chill factor." If people are ignoring your intelligence, and the Pentagon and NSC keep telling you, "What about this? What about this? Keep looking!"—well, then you start focusing on one thing instead of the other thing, because you know that's what your political masters want to hear.[7]

The concerns over repeated questioning even made their way to DCI Tenet, who wrote in his autobiography,

> [S]ome of our analysts, junior and senior, chafed at the constant drumbeat of repetitive queries on Iraq and al-Qa'ida. Jami Miscik, our senior analyst, came to me one day in mid-2002 complaining that several policy makers, notably Scooter Libby and Paul Wolfowitz, never seemed satisfied with our answers regarding allegations of Iraqi complicity with al-Qa'ida.[8]

In journalist Ron Suskind's book on the War on Terror, Miscik said, "What became apparent . . . is that some questions kept getting asked over and over and over again . . . as if, somehow, the answer would change, even without any good reason for it to change—like any new information coming in."[9]

Tenet himself noted how repeated questioning affected the IC: "The vice president and others pushed us hard on this issue, and our answers never satisfied him or some of our other regular 'customers.' Paul Wolfowitz and

---

[6]   Rovner, 2011, p. 149.

[7]   As quoted in Robert Dreyfuss, "The Pentagon Muzzles the CIA," *American Prospect*, November 21, 2002.

[8]   Tenet and Harlow, 2007, p. 302.

[9]   Suskind, 2006, p. 124.

Scooter Libby, for example, were relentless in asking us to check, recheck, and recheck."[10] During an interview with RAND researchers, one former IC official noted that the decisionmaking process always involves some degree of give and take between analysts and policymakers. This official said that some analysts do not like to be challenged and would interpret it as an attempt to influence the decision.[11] However, former National Intelligence Officer Paul Pillar noted that the motivation behind the repeated questioning matters:

> Directing concentrated attention to the topics of most concern to policymakers is an entirely legitimate response by intelligence agencies. But in this instance the purpose of the enormous amount of work devoted to the policymakers' preferred lines of inquiry was not to help them make better-informed decisions, but instead to help them sell the war decision to the public. This role was not a legitimate one for an intelligence service.[12]

As Pillar notes, the motivation behind the repeated questioning on the issue of links between Iraq and al Qaeda was not to improve intelligence; it was an effort on the part of policymakers to receive intelligence that could be used for other purposes—in this case, bolstering the public relations effort to make the war tenable for the American public. Because analysts are inherently sensitive to the needs of policymakers (it is the core mission of intelligence to provide information to those in a position to make decisions), repeated questioning was a way of indirectly biasing estimates. However, it is important to note that the IC never changed its estimation that there were minimal links between Iraq and al Qaeda.

---

[10] Tenet and Harlow, 2007, p. 342.

[11] Former senior IC leader, interview with the authors.

[12] Pillar, 2011, p. 165.

Policy Officials Disseminating Intelligence Analyses

In looking to spread the allegation that Hussein's Iraq had substantial ties to al Qaeda, Under Secretary of Defense Douglas Feith established a small DoD unit called the Policy Counter Terrorism Evaluation Group (PCTEG). Feith, supposedly at the urging of Wolfowitz, created PCTEG in an effort to gather as much material as possible about links between Iraq and al Qaeda to use in the public relations campaign. Feith also used PCTEG to attempt to discredit the IC's judgment that no such links existed.[13] This is telling in relation to bias for two reasons: first, because a policy official (Feith) used a policy organization to aggregate and analyze intelligence (although the analysis was suspect), and second, because by disseminating such dubious reports, policy officials were undercutting the executive branch's IC, which is charged with making objective assessments.

The degree to which PCTEG's work had no foundation with intelligence is illustrated in a briefing that the group gave to DCI Tenet. From the beginning of the presentation, which was titled "Iraq and al-Qa'ida—Making the Case," Tenet knew that the policy group was doing something inappropriate. Tenet wrote that "[Tina Shelton] started out by saying that there should be 'no more debate' on the Iraq–al-Qa'ida relationship. 'It is an open-and-shut case,' she said. 'No further analysis is required.'" Shelton, the naval reservist on Feith's team, went on to say that the terror group and Iraq had a "mature, symbiotic relationship." Reflecting on the briefing, Tenet wrote, "This was one of my rare moments of trying to be subtle. What I was really thinking was, This is complete crap, and I want this to end right now."[14] Tenet pulled Vice Admiral Jake Jacoby, the chief of DIA, out of the meeting, and said, "This is entirely inappropriate. You get this back in intelligence channels. I want analysts talking to analysts, not people with agendas."[15] Furthermore, regarding the PCTEG team, Tenet wrote, "Trouble was, while they seemed

---

[13] Pillar, 2011.

[14] Tenet, 2007, pp. 347–348.

[15] Tenet, 2007, p. 348.

to like playing the role of analysts, they showed none of the professional skills or discipline required."[16]

The role of PCTEG was actually more substantial; Tenet later found out that the group had been briefing the White House, the NSC, and officials from the Office of the Vice President. Moreover, CIA officials, including Paul Pillar and Ben Bonk, learned at a Senate Select Committee on Intelligence hearing that Feith's unit had been adding a slide at the end of the presentation for policy officials. That slide was titled, "Fundamental Problems with How Intelligence Community is Assessing Information."[17] PCTEG came to have an outsized influence on the Bush administration's public campaign for the war. According to Pillar,

> The case was fabricated during the year-long prewar sales campaign but reached a climax several months into the war, when the *Weekly Standard* published a list, compiled by the unit Douglas Feith had created in the Pentagon, of alleged contacts between Iraq and al-Qa'ida. Cheney completed the circle in this circular sourcing in an interview a few weeks later when he commended the leaked compilation in the *Weekly Standard* as the "best source of information" on the subject.[18]

The result of this episode was that the Bush administration used information masquerading as intelligence from a unit whose primary mission was to support policy rather than provide objective analysis in an effort to make the Iraq War more palatable to the American people.

Public Statements Not Supported by Intelligence

With the administration actively using intelligence to build support for war, officials naturally included specific details in public statements. The problem, however, was that the statements did not always comport with the foundational intelligence. There were multiple instances in which admin-

---

[16] Tenet, 2007, p. 347.

[17] Pillar, 2011, p. 47.

[18] Pillar, 2011, pp. 145–146.

istration officials manipulated or stretched intelligence beyond reasonable means to support certain policy positions. In this section, we review the discussion surrounding Iraq and WMD. Rovner highlights several of these instances: Vice President Dick Cheney claimed that Iraq was "clearly pursuing these deadly capabilities," Secretary of Defense Donald Rumsfeld argued that there was "no question" that Iraq was bolstering its production of WMD, and Secretary of State Colin Powell said that Iraq was diverting oil revenues to develop chemical, biological, and nuclear weapons.[19] There are two particularly telling episodes in which this form of bias manifested: the inclusion of the "16 words" in President Bush's State of the Union address on uranium ore in Niger and National Security Adviser Condoleezza Rice's successful efforts to make DCI Tenet "clarify" certain remarks so they did not diverge from the policy line.

The 16 words in President Bush's State of the Union address were that "[t]he British Government has learned that Saddam Hussein recently sought significant quantities of uranium from Africa."[20] Before the speech, Bush administration officials repeatedly tried to include reports about Iraq attempting to purchase uranium ore in Niger. The IC convinced Rice to delete a reference from a presidential statement about Iraq, and the CIA was successful in removing the line from a speech on Iraq in Cincinnati in October 2002. For the Cincinnati speech, DCI Tenet directly called Deputy National Security Adviser Steve Hadley to lay out the problems. In a memo to Hadley, Tenet wrote, "Remove the sentence because the amount is in dispute and it is debatable whether [uranium oxide] can be acquired from the source. We told Congress that the Brits have exaggerated this issue. Finally, the Iraqis already have 550 metric tons of uranium oxide in their inventory."[21] A senior analyst sent another memo the next day outlining additional problems with this Cincinnati speech.

Despite repeated warnings about the uranium ore, the White House was finally successful in including the language in the 2003 State of the Union.

---

[19] As quoted in Rovner, 2011, p. 149.

[20] George W. Bush, "Address Before a Joint Session of the Congress on the State of the Union," January 28, 2003.

[21] Tenet, 2007, p. 450.

The administration was able to do so by attributing the report to the British.[22] Pillar, with regard to National Security Adviser Rice's later recriminations over the episode, wrote that she argued as follows: "'You failed to prevent us from misusing intelligence when, despite your repeated previous efforts and warnings, we insisted on doing so.' Or, more succinctly, 'It's your fault because you didn't keep us from misbehaving.'"[23] Pillar continued, "The intelligence community thus came to be judged not only for whether it got things right, but also for how vigorously it resisted when policymakers insisted on getting things wrong."[24] Although it received the most attention, the flap over the 16 words was not the only instance in which public statements by administration officials created issues with the IC.

In October 2002, news reports started discussing divisions between the IC and the administration with regard to Iraq's WMD and the country's link to al Qaeda. According to *The New York Times,*

---

[22] Pillar discusses the way in which the line was finally included:

> The NSC's senior nonproliferation official, Robert Joseph, called Alan Foley, the chief of the intelligence community's nonproliferation center, and proposed that the report be cited while attributing it to the British. Foley's acquiescence was the reaction of an intelligence officer accustomed to dealing with many reports of uncertain credibility and being comfortable doing so as long as the sourcing was specified and unjustified conclusions were not explicitly built on them. It was not the reaction of someone wise in the ways of speechwriting gamesmanship and the public manipulation of images (Pillar, 2011, pp. 33–34).

[23] Pillar, 2011, p. 34.

[24] Pillar, 2011, p. 35. The episode over the 16 words became politically pointed after Ambassador Joe Wilson published a column in *The New York Times* titled "What I Didn't Find in Africa." Wilson had been tapped in February 2002 to visit Niger and investigate whether there was any substance to earlier allegations about sales of uranium to Iraq. Wilson discussed the matter with local officials in Niger, who denied selling uranium to Iraq but did mention that they were seeking expanded trade relations with the Middle Eastern country. After President Bush made the comments in the State of the Union, Wilson fed reports to several journalists, wrote the op-ed, and then appeared as a guest on television program *Meet the Press* to discuss his findings about the relationship between Niger and Iraq. This episode became even more politicized after journalists leaked the name of Wilson's wife, CIA officer Valerie Plame. Investigations into the leak ultimately led to Vice President Cheney's chief of staff Scooter Libby being charged with perjury.

A letter to Congress from the director of central intelligence has brought into public view divisions within the administration over what intelligence shows about Iraq's intentions and its willingness to ally itself with Al Qaeda. The letter and other reports from the C.I.A. paint a worrisome picture of Iraq's pursuit of nuclear and other weapons of mass destruction. But they do not support the White House's view that Iraq presents an immediate threat to the American homeland and may use Al Qaeda to carry out attacks at any moment.[25]

More specifically, the division referred to the part of the National Intelligence Estimate (NIE) that argued that Hussein would use WMDs only if he was directly threatened by the United States. This contrasted with the administration's view, which argued that the weapons posed an immediate threat. The day before the article came out, White House press secretary Ari Fleischer gave a briefing in which he was asked about differences between the administration and the CIA with regard to the NIE on Iraq's weapons. Fleischer said, "No, they're one and the same, as Director Tenet said. Director Tenet has said that there is a similar approach, and it's based on the analysis that has been provided to the President."[26]

Administration officials quickly sought to diminish any appearance of disunity. DCI Tenet received what he described as a "frantic call" from Rice, who wanted him to "clarify" the issue immediately. In what he later recognized as a mistake, Tenet met with the *Times* reporter. Tenet told the reporter, "There was no inconsistency in the views in the letter and those of the president." According to Tenet, "[b]y making public comments in the middle of a contentious political debate, I gave the impression that I was becoming a partisan player."[27] This pressure from the administration to "clarify" the letter shows the degree to which officials were using the intelligence to sell the war. More importantly, administration officials were using DCI Tenet as part of the public relations campaign, even though there were

---

[25] Michael R. Gordon, "Threats and Responses: Intelligence—U.S. Aides Split on Assessment of Iraq's Plans," *New York Times*, October 10, 2002.

[26] Ari Fleischer, "Press Briefing by Ari Fleischer," The American Presidency Project, October 9, 2002.

[27] Tenet, 2007, p. 336.

differences in the IC's analytical line and the evidence that policymakers were citing as justification for invasion.

Retaliation Against Those with Alternative Viewpoints

A common refrain in interviews with intelligence officials serving under more recent administrations was a reticence to speak up on matters they knew would displease the policymakers. Analysts would get bullied and withdraw, always with the knowledge that offering a dissenting opinion was a good way to not be invited to future meetings. This phenomenon also occurred in the early 2000s, when members of the IC and military faced repercussions for not supporting the policy line during Bush's time in office. According to Pillar, "Not only was there no assessment of relevant and available information and images, but the war makers also consciously and forcefully rejected them. Those with contrary insights were not just ignored but punished."[28]

Pillar cited two individuals whom he believed suffered retaliation for their contrary analyses. First was the DIA officer for the Middle East, Bruce Hardcastle. In Michael Isikoff and David Corn's account of the Iraq War, Hardcastle said, "You were never told what to write. . . . But you knew what assessments administration officials would be receptive to—and what they would not be receptive to."[29] Former Clinton adviser Sidney Blumenthal

---

[28] Pillar, 2011, p. 67.

[29] Quoted in Michael Isikoff and David Corn, *Hubris: The Inside Story of Spin, Scandal, and the Selling of the Iraq War*, New York: Three Rivers Press, 2006, pp. 135–136.

Hardcastle's relationship with Deputy Under Secretary William Luti became the focus of a *Washington Post* article by Thomas Ricks. Luti insisted that the Middle East policy office was a "consumer of intelligence rather than a provider," which does "policy work" and is concerned with "developing defense policy options and monitoring their implementation—not collecting intelligence, planning wars or implementing policy." According to Ricks, "Hardcastle . . . began avoiding meeting with Luti after sharply disagreeing with him over the past 12 months about the imminence of the threat posed by Saddam Hussein's Iraq." Furthermore, Ricks quoted a Pentagon official who said, "It's very difficult to inform people who already know it all" and a former DIA analyst who said, "[b]asically, he [Luti] didn't like other people's information if it didn't agree with

wrote a *Sydney Morning Herald* article in 2004 discussing what happened to Hardcastle once he offered an assessment to which policymakers were not receptive. Blumenthal quotes former CIA official Patrick Lang, who said that Hardcastle told Bush administration officials "that the way they were handling evidence was wrong." In response, Hardcastle was not simply removed from his position; "[t]hey did away with his job. . . . They wanted only liaison officers . . . not a senior intelligence person who argued with them."[30] According to Pillar, "Bruce himself clashed sufficiently with Feith's deputies for him to be consigned to the wilderness and not invited to meetings someone in his position normally would be expected to attend."[31]

The second individual Pillar cited as facing repercussions for providing unwelcome assessments was Army Chief of Staff Eric Shinseki. Shinseki's troubles with the Bush administration started when he gave testimony to the Senate Armed Services Committee on February 25, 2003 (a month before the Iraq invasion started). When asked how many troops would be needed after the invasion, Shinseki said,

> Something on the order of several hundred thousand soldiers are probably . . . a figure that would be required. . . . We're talking about post-hostilities control over a piece of geography that's fairly significant, with the kinds of ethnic tensions that could lead to other problems. . . . It takes a significant ground force presence to maintain a safe and secure environment, to ensure that people are fed, that water is distributed, all the normal responsibilities that go along with administering a situation like this.[32]

In testimony a few days later, Wolfowitz would say that Shinseki's estimate (which later turned out to be substantively correct) was "wildly off the mark." Secretary of Defense Rumsfeld would similarly say, "The idea

---

his opinion" (Thomas E. Ricks, "Iraq War Planner Downplays Role," *Washington Post*, October 22, 2003).

[30] Sidney Blumenthal, "Spies Toed Iraq Line, or Fell to the Hawks," *Sydney Morning Herald*, February 9, 2004.

[31] Pillar, 2011, p. 160.

[32] Myleftnutmegblog, "Gen. Eric Shinseki from 02.25.03," video, YouTube, December 7, 2008.

that it would take several hundred thousand U.S. forces I think is far off the mark."[33] For providing the dissenting analysis, Shinseki was "first vilified, then marginalized by the Bush administration."[34] According to Pillar, "Rumsfeld and Wolfowitz subsequently sidelined Shinseki as a lame duck through the unprecedented tactic of announcing his successor eighteen months in advance and further snubbed him by boycotting his retirement ceremony."[35] George Packer also discussed the episode, noting that "[t] he cost of dissent was humiliation and professional suicide."[36] Moreover, Rumsfeld and Wolfowitz's treatment of Shinseki rippled through the ranks. One Air Force officer involved in the planning said, "After seeing Wolfowitz chew down a four-star, I don't think anyone was going to raise their head up and make a stink about it."[37] The way in which Bush administration officials retaliated against high-ranking officials who offered dissenting analyses clearly introduced biased intelligence assessments. As Hardcastle and the Air Force officer said, dissenting analyses were not welcomed by policymakers. Because the IC depends on policymakers for its entrée, analysts had a clear incentive (both personally and professionally) to toe the policy line.

Intelligence Community Self-Adjustments

In the face of repeated questioning, intelligence briefings from policy officials, the constant struggle with public statements, and the retaliation against dissenters, analysts quickly recognized what the policy line was and what would happen to those who did not support it. The IC started making self-adjustments to ensure that it stayed relevant for decisionmakers. It must be recognized, however, that these self-adjustments were limited. Although

---

[33] Quoted in Eric Schmitt, "Threats and Responses: Military Spending; Pentagon Contradicts General on Iraq Occupation Force's Size," *New York Times*, February 28, 2003.

[34] Thom Shanker, "New Strategy Vindicates Ex-Army Chief Shinseki," *New York Times*, January 12, 2007.

[35] Pillar, 2011, p. 52.

[36] George Packer, *The Assassins' Gate: America in Iraq*, New York: Farrar, Straus and Giroux, 2005, p. 117.

[37] As quoted in Packer, 2005, p. 117, and Pillar, 2011, p. 52.

the IC did change the way in which it considered and presented evidence on Iraq's WMD, it never acceded to pressure with regard to the links between Iraq and al Qaeda. Most analysts say that they did not change analyses in response to political suasion, but Jack Davis, a longtime CIA analyst and expert on analytical methodology, discussed how the consistent pressure subconsciously affects the intelligence product. Davis wrote that

> [a]nalysts . . . admit to the presence of policy pressures but tend to deny that the pressures have an effect on their judgements. Yet there is evidence in postmortem reports and academic studies that analysts, in making judgments amid uncertainty at a subconscious level, often are influenced by knowledge of the policy preference of either or both the administration and Congress.[38]

Even beyond the subconscious, psychological pressures, administration officials actively worked to change IC findings. After the CIA wrote a report showing very few links between Iraq and al Qaeda, Tenet wrote that CIA analysts received "a series of calls from the White House . . . to revise or withdraw the paper."[39] In another episode, Deputy National Security Adviser Stephen Hadley told CIA analysts that the case for Iraq and WMD needed to be "beefed up."[40] President Bush himself had similar reactions to intelligence. After a briefing on Iraq's WMD from Deputy DCI John McLaughlin, President Bush said, "Nice try . . . [but] it's not something that Joe Public would understand or would gain a lot of confidence from."[41] Facing this level of resistance from policymakers, IC analysts made self-adjustments to stay relevant to the administration. Such adjustments included removing language reflecting the uncertainty of the intelligence. The CIA also started to downplay the overall lack of information to present

---

[38] Jack Davis, "Why Bad Things Happen to Good Analysts," *Studies in Intelligence,* Vol. 60, No. 3, September 2016, p. 21.

[39] Tenet, 2007, p. 349.

[40] Tenet, 2007, p. 371.

[41] This episode is recounted in Pillar, 2011, p. 32, and Tenet, 2007, p. 361.

a more concrete picture.[42] According to Rovner, "the tenor of intelligence briefings to White House officials also changed ... [becoming] more certain about Iraqi capabilities and intentions, despite continuing doubts among analysts."[43] Although the underlying bits of intelligence did not change, the IC altered the way that it presented and discussed the information, allowing policymakers to make the case for the war with a greater deal of certainty than the data warranted.

Conclusion

In summary, intelligence products in the lead-up to the Iraq War were heavily biased for several reasons. Bush administration officials repeatedly questioned specific findings, policy officials started disseminating their own intelligence briefings, public statements used unreliable information, and those offering dissenting opinions were cast aside. In the face of these pressures, the IC made several course corrections of its own, presenting intelligence without the language of ambiguity or uncertainty that it required. Although memoirs of IC officials and later scholarly reviews reached the consensus that the Iraq War would have happened regardless of the intelligence, they also found that the intelligence was instrumental in garnering public support for the invasion.

---

[42] Rovner, 2011, pp. 150–152, discusses adjustments the IC made to adapt to policymakers' preferences.

[43] Rovner, 2011, p. 151.

CHAPTER SEVEN

The Obama Administration (2009–2017)

Since 9/11, U.S. national security policy has been defined by the war on terrorism: in Afghanistan, Iraq, and elsewhere around the world. As Barack Obama was beginning his presidency in 2008, he "inherited an IC facing a contradictory situation."[1] The IC's analytic line was under scrutiny in lieu of recent "failures," fueling a "growing public mistrust of intelligence agencies."[2] In particular, one participant observed that the American public saw IC contributions to the Cold War as valued and important, but this view became marred following the IC's role in the assessment of Iraq's WMD. According to one interviewee, the "debacle after 9/11 was a huge hit to the IC."[3] However, the IC maintained authorities and resources under post-9/11 national security and counterterrorism reforms "like never before."[4]

In this environment, the IC faced challenges with the public and policymakers during the Obama administration. While it was focused on the Global War on Terror, the IC became involved in the investigation into the September 2012 attack in Benghazi, Libya, and the administration's promise to close the Guantanamo Bay detention facility in Cuba. At the same time, the IC's role in domestic policy issues became more public following

---

[1] Charlotte Lepri, "Obama's Intelligence Policy: Meeting New Challenges," in Bahram M. Rajaee and Mark J. Miller, eds., *National Security Under the Obama Administration*, New York: Palgrave Macmillan, 2012, p. 63.

[2] Lepri, 2012, p. 63.

[3] Former senior official, interview with the authors.

[4] Lepri, 2012, p. 63.

Edward Snowden's unauthorized disclosure of intelligence information and the influx of unaccompanied children at the U.S. southwest border.

Furthermore, the perception of bias across intelligence agencies persisted. For example, one interview participant recounted the timing of a speech President Obama gave on al Qaeda, which occurred toward the end of his presidency and during the transition to the new administration and inadvertently coincided with the PDB the IC wrote on the topic of al Qaeda's abilities. Some senior White House officials thought that the PDB was intended to undermine the outgoing President and favor the incoming President, Donald Trump.[5] Although the PDB authors might not have known about the speech, the interview participant (who said that politicization was not a factor in this case) noted that the IC's internal review process helped create a perception that bias existed.[6]

Bias During the Obama Administration

Some interviewees observed that cultural and policy biases would manifest at times in the IC.[7] Cultural biases were especially evident in the disconnect between incentives for IC analysts for "speaking truth to power" and positive feedback for the information they provided to policymakers.[8] No analyst has been rewarded for receiving negative feedback on their work, and there is no structure whereby the IC gets rewarded for "speaking truth to power."[9] John Gentry wrote that the IC did not speak much truth to President Obama, despite the perception that his foreign policy was controversial. However, Gentry noted that the IC did have a positive attitude toward the President, despite divergent views on such issues as the CIA's

---

[5] Former senior official, interview with the authors.

[6] Former senior official, interview with the authors.

[7] Multiple senior officials, interviews with the authors.

[8] Former senior official, interview with the authors.

[9] Former senior official, interview with the authors.

"enhanced interrogation" program.[10] Speaking truth to power also can be difficult when policymakers feel that the truth is always going to be "bad news;" warnings that they will not be able to achieve their objectives instead of opportunities that the policymakers can leverage to attain them.[11]

Furthermore, according to RAND interviews with multiple senior officials, the definition of *useful* from a policymaker's perspective differs from that of an IC official. In some instances, directors would include or pick information according to what they thought their policymaker customer wanted to see (see examples in the next section, on self-censorship).[12] Some interview participants indicated that there is an inherent tension between the views of the IC and those of the policymakers.[13] The primary source of this tension is the difference between how the IC analyzes problems and the context of policymaker deliberations, which the IC might not understand. Policymakers have a close relationship with the people and issues that shape policy agendas and look for certainty when trying to obtain their policy objectives. However, the IC is not well equipped to provide that certainty. Rather, the IC is insulated from the same people and issues to avoid compromising its objectivity, which policymakers view as refusal to understand or incorporate the views of decisionmakers into IC assessments.[14] Interview participants also agreed that proper relationships between intelligence agencies and policymakers had not yet been established.[15]

Overall, interview participants revealed mixed perspectives regarding the existence of internal biases within the IC. While some did not observe any internal bias because of leadership behavior or analytic processes, others noted cultural, policy, and analytic biases. One interviewee stated that they

---

[10] John A. Gentry, "'Truth' as a Tool of the Politicization of Intelligence," *International Journal of Intelligence and CounterIntelligence*, Vol. 32, No. 2, 2019b, p. 224.

[11] James B. Steinberg, "The Policymaker's Perspective: Transparency and Partnership," in Roger Z. George and James B. Bruce, eds., *Analyzing Intelligence: National Security Practitioners' Perspectives*, 2nd ed., Washington, D.C.: Georgetown University Press, 2014, pp. 95–96.

[12] Former senior official, interview with the authors.

[13] Former senior officials, interviews with the authors.

[14] Steinberg, 2014, p. 96.

[15] Former senior official, interview with the authors.

did not perceive any internal bias because the "agency leadership did not override local area experts."[16] Another interviewee remembered that internal bias was not part of their life as an analyst or as a policymaker, that they "just never saw it."[17] This view was prevalent among analysts in the counterterrorism community, where participants attributed the lack of internal bias to "more uniformity of view" on certain issues.[18] That view, however, sometimes depended on the country and extremist group.

On the other hand, external bias sometimes did appear, albeit in less obvious ways. One interview participant noted that some members of the Obama administration had a more strategic approach in the way in which they interacted with the IC.[19] These members requested such intelligence products as the NIE to help change the focus or shift the debate, for example. At the same time, one interview participant admitted that they did not have official conversations about bias with senior personnel from the IC, but they also never received any secret requests to "re-do" analysis, only to probe facts or analytic lines.[20]

Finally, one interview participant held the view that "biases arise when external pressures intervene, or processes are not allowed to progress unimpeded," and that bias in the IC is not a systemic problem.[21] The problem is external and needs hardening.[22] The system established within the IC is not failing but being intentionally undermined by outside forces.[23]

---

[16] Former senior official, interview with the authors.

[17] Former senior official, interview with the authors.

[18] Former senior official, interview with the authors.

[19] Former senior official, interview with the authors.

[20] Former senior official, interview with the authors.

[21] Former senior official, interview with the authors.

[22] Former senior official, interview with the authors.

[23] Former senior official, interview with the authors.

Internal Bias: "Politicization by Omission" or Self-Censorship

"Politicization by omission" or self-censorship is one example of internal bias. Gentry described his personal experience at DIA during the Obama presidency, when editors of the agency's primary intelligence publication told the analysts to avoid "specifically identified terms that might trigger criticism of administration policy."[24] Gentry also remembered that this "policy of politicization provoked no apparent reaction" from the analytic corps. In his own research, Gentry found that during Obama's presidency, intelligence analysis suffered from "politicization by omission"—leaving out issues from regular updates or assessments "because the results might displease superiors."[25]

One interview participant observed that after former National Security Agency (NSA) contractor Edward Snowden's 2013 unauthorized disclosure of U.S. surveillance programs, analysts were "much less willing to discuss their sources in reporting cables and were careful in criticizing individuals."[26] Although the "thrust of their analysis came through," it was much less rich.[27]

A year later, former CIA director Michael Hayden wrote that the IC "was slow to recognize Russia's growing information operations in the United States in 2014" and did not begin to take notice until 2015, as the 2016 presidential election was approaching.[28] Hayden noted that the IC knew that President Obama had been trying to reset relations with Russia and did not regard Russia as a major issue.[29] Intelligence analysts also knew that

---

[24] John A. Gentry, "A New Form of Politicization? Has the CIA Become Institutionally Biased or Politicized?" *International Journal of Intelligence and CounterIntelligence*, Vol. 31, No. 4, 2018, p. 661.

[25] Robert Jervis, "Why Intelligence and Policymakers Clash," *Political Science Quarterly*, Vol. 125, No. 2, Summer 2010b, p. 200.

[26] Former senior official, interview with the authors.

[27] Former senior official, interview with the authors.

[28] John A. Gentry, "Partisan Political Polemics: Wrecking One's Reputation," *International Journal of Intelligence and CounterIntelligence*, Vol. 32, No. 1, 2019a, p. 174.

[29] Gentry, 2019a, p. 174.

national security interests at the time lay in counterterrorism intelligence. Gentry quoted Hayden's assessment of this type of IC response to administration policy as "a subtle form of self-censorship" or "self-policing."[30]

In 2015, the IC fielded an annual Analytic Objectivity and Process Survey.[31] Sixty-five percent of U.S. Central Command (CENTCOM) responses to a free text question in the survey indicated the following reasons their analysis was distorted or suppressed in the face of evidence: (1) analytic or editorial disagreement, (2) politicization, or (3) not matched with the existing analytic line.[32] Themes associated with protecting agency interests and not wanting to offend stakeholders occurred in 10 percent and 3 percent of the responses, respectively. Although the latter proportions of responses were relatively low, they indicated the presence of some level of self-censorship, at least within CENTCOM.

The practice of self-censorship during President Obama's tenure occurred in different areas of the IC and for different reasons, suggesting that it was not institutionalized. Furthermore, the available evidence shows that this practice was small in scale. Post-Snowden analysts were more protective of their sources and refrained from criticizing individuals but did not alter their assessments. The IC eventually turned its attention to Russia's information operations against U.S. presidential elections, and the distortion or suppression of analysis in CENTCOM began to be reported only after General James Mattis and his senior intelligence leaders departed in 2013.[33] However, even as self-censorship practices popped up sporadically, they showed that intelligence analysts remained sensitive to issues that could externally influence assessments.

---

[30] Gentry, 2019a, p. 175.

[31] Office of the Director of National Intelligence (ODNI), "Objectivity," webpage, undated b.

[32] ODNI, "(U) Selected CENTCOM Respondent Descriptions from the FY2015 AOPS," October 17, 2016. This is part of the same survey cited by the Joint Task Force created by the Chairman of the House Armed Services Committee, the House Permanent Select Committee on Intelligence, and the House Appropriations Subcommittee on Defense to investigate CENTCOM intelligence analysis in 2016.

[33] U.S. House of Representatives, *(U) Initial Findings of the U.S. House of Representatives Joint Task Force on U.S. Central Command Intelligence Analysis*, August 10, 2016, p. 1.

External Bias in Counterterrorism and Green Forces Analysis

Our interview analysis revealed that external bias can appear in different ways in the counterterrorism space. Although interviewees noted that internal bias among counterterrorism analysts was rare, there are examples of external bias and pressures, such as (1) policymakers' preference for one IC agency's counterterrorism analysis over another's to support their own goals in this space and (2) a particular preference for one agency over another for its analysis of green forces.[34]

Counterterrorism: Central Intelligence Agency Versus Defense Intelligence Agency

We found that internal bias did not appear to be prevalent among analysts in the counterterrorism community, but that "biases arise when external pressures intervene," according to one interviewee.[35] We also found that policymakers actively used the IC to support their own strategic goals. In this section, we discuss how policymakers' preferences for analysis produced by certain intelligence agencies can create the perception of bias in counterterrorism analysis.

According to one interviewee, policymakers perceived that the CIA's and, to some extent, DIA's analyses became "more sensitive to operational considerations."[36] Policymakers were more skeptical of estimates from the CIA and from the military regarding the status of counterterrorism efforts and groups and the efficacy of counterterrorism operations against those groups. For example, it was hard to separate the analytic line from operational realities, particularly around estimates on al Qaeda senior leadership and the efficacy of counterterrorism operations in certain countries. Our interviewees observed that for analysts, "marrying the analytic and opera-

---

[34] *Green forces* refers to those forces fighting side by side with blue forces in a temporary alliance. *Blue forces* are friendly forces, including those allied by treaty. *Red forces* are enemy forces.

[35] Former senior official, interview with the authors.

[36] Former senior official, interview with the authors.

tional lines [was] challenging."[37] In response, some within the IC saw the need for the National Counterterrorism Center to take the lead for counterterrorism estimates to avoid having an operational agency leading this effort. Although policymakers could have benefited from operational agencies' estimates, some analysts in the IC did not trust that the operational agencies would be entirely objective.

Furthermore, some interview participants admitted their own preferences for receiving information from certain intelligence agencies. When they received information from DIA, for example, they would seek out CIA analysis because they did not completely trust DIA's analytic line.[38] One interview participant observed that policymakers have the freedom to "shop around" for the analytic viewpoint that better supports their policy aims.[39] However, this freedom of choice might negatively affect the IC by propagating external bias. Showing preference for one IC agency's assessment over another could build the perception that one IC agency is more trustworthy than another or more supportive of a particular policy. Additionally, rather than basing policy on all available information across the IC, by shopping around, policymakers seek out only that information that most suits their policy goals, thereby making it seem as though a particular agency supports those goals.

Green Forces Analysis: The Central Intelligence Agency Versus the Defense Intelligence Agency

Those policymakers who preferred CIA's analytic line also admitted that their preference was particularly influenced by analysis of green forces. One interview participant explained it this way: DIA might not have had a "clear eye view of what was happening on the ground," because their military command structure was trying to establish a close working relationship with the organization that the IC was going to analyze.[40] Thus,

---

[37] Former senior official, interview with the authors.

[38] Former senior official, interview with the authors.

[39] Former senior official, interview with the authors.

[40] Former senior official, interview with the authors.

DIA could not "clearly articulate [the] capabilities" of their partners on the ground.[41] In this instance, the source of external bias was the combatant commander's view of "what success is."[42] For example, assessing the capability of the Afghan National Defense and Security Forces (ANDSF) and the blue force assisting the ANDSF "was messy."[43] The intelligence policy on estimating the effectiveness of operational assistance and the ANDSF's mission to train, advise, and assist "was not effective for anyone, nobody trusted anyone's viewpoint."[44] Those in the field were interested in a different outcome.

This situation was similar to that of the Iraqi Security Forces (ISF). Our interviewees stated that combatant command (COCOM) intelligence products and command and control structures on the ground are good at tactics and tactical insights but are less sophisticated and are biased about intelligence analysis more broadly.[45] For example, in 2014, a whistleblower alleged that CENTCOM manipulated the intelligence it produced to present an "unduly positive outlook on CENTCOM efforts to train the ISF and combat the self-proclaimed Islamic State of Iraq and the Levant (ISIL)."[46] The investigation of the Joint Task Force (JTF), created by the Chairman of the House Armed Services Committee, the House Permanent Select Committee on Intelligence, and the House Appropriations Subcommittee on Defense, found that "CENTCOM's analytic positions were more positive regarding the efforts to combat [the Islamic State of Iraq and Syria (ISIS)] than those of the IC elements."[47] James Clapper, who was Director of National Intelligence in 2014, also admitted that the IC underestimated ISIS and overestimated the ISF's ability to hold Iraq after the United States withdrew its forc-

---

[41] Former senior official, interview with the authors.

[42] Former senior official, interview with the authors.

[43] Former senior official, interview with the authors.

[44] Former senior official, interview with the authors.

[45] Former senior official, interview with the authors.

[46] ISIL is also known as the Islamic State of Iraq and Syria (ISIS); U.S. House of Representatives, 2016, p. 1.

[47] U.S. House of Representatives, 2016, p. i.

es.[48] CENTCOM intelligence products, public statements, and testimonies were inconsistent with both the judgments of many senior career analysts at CENTCOM and the actual events at the time.[49] For example, CENTCOM leaders claimed in public statements and testimonies that "ISIL is on the defense," is in a "defensive crouch," and "is losing ground," while Intelligence Directorate senior leaders whom the JTF interviewed "indicated this characterization did not reflect their best assessments at the time."[50] After the CENTCOM statements were made, ISIL overran the ISF positions in Ramadi, causing the ISF to retreat. Additionally, according to survey results the JTF obtained from the Office of the Director of National Intelligence (ODNI) during its investigation, 40 percent of the analysts said, "they had experienced an attempt to distort or suppress intelligence in the past year."[51]

One interview participant also spoke about external bias emanating from COCOMs over an assessment of Yemen in 2011.[52] Those perceptions sharpened when a COCOM's estimative wing was the lead author on an assessment. According to the interviewee, it became difficult "to separate out objective analysis from the military line." This line of thinking continued when Lieutenant General Michael Flynn took command of DIA in July 2012. To one interview participant, General Flynn's appointment helped reaffirm old prejudices; Flynn was seen as "working to distort information to fit his own biases."[53] Another participant pointed out that sometimes, if DIA was the lead drafter of a report, that report tended to reflect the DoD point of view.[54] This observation did not necessarily point to pressure from senior military officers or from the Joint Staff, but non-DoD IC analysts perceived a bias in the DoD view when reviewing those products.

---

[48] Office of the Press Secretary, "Press Briefing by Press Secretary Josh Earnest, 12/8/16," Washington, D.C.: Obama White House Archives, December 8, 2016.

[49] U.S. House of Representatives, 2016, p. 1.

[50] U.S. House of Representatives, 2016, p. 1.

[51] U.S. House of Representatives, 2016, p. 1.

[52] Former senior official, interview with the authors.

[53] Former senior official, interview with the authors.

[54] Former senior official, interview with the authors.

Intelligence analysis is very difficult to apply to green forces analysis and comes "very close to analytic bias," according to one interviewee.[55] The interviews that observed the tension between intelligence analysis and operational realities in counterterrorism operations echoed a similar sentiment. Trying to evaluate the effectiveness of a close institutional or operational partner introduced a biased intelligence perspective; at the same time, assessing the effectiveness of blue forces in counterterrorism operations during a protracted war created the perception of external bias. Our interview participants concluded that the IC has not been able to resolve this issue.

External Bias in Talking Points

One interview participant discussed the development of talking points as another area where external bias creeped into the work of the IC, creating the "most intense" friction between the IC and policymakers.[56] Sometimes, this friction was subtle, and it was up to the IC "to hold the line" on what was appropriate to say. The Senate Intelligence Committee's declassified, bipartisan report on the Benghazi terrorist attacks found that "the intelligence picture after the attacks contributed to the controversial CIA talking points," referencing intelligence reports after September 11, 2012, in which "intelligence analysts inaccurately referred to the presence of a protest at the U.S. mission facility before the attack."[57] The Committee also concluded that the IC took too long to correct these erroneous reports, "which caused confusion and influenced the public statements of policymakers."[58]

More than two weeks after the attacks, ODNI released a statement explaining that preliminary analysis of available information "led us to assess that the attack began spontaneously" following protests at the U.S.

---

[55] Former senior official, interview with the authors.

[56] Former senior official, interview with the authors.

[57] U.S. Senate Select Committee on Intelligence, "Senate Intelligence Committee Releases Declassified Bipartisan Report on Benghazi Terrorist Attacks," press release, January 15, 2014.

[58] U.S. Senate Select Committee on Intelligence, 2014.

embassy in Cairo in response to a film that ridiculed the Prophet Muhammad and Islam.[59] The talking points that were provided to the House Permanent Select Committee on Intelligence for use with the media on September 14, 2012, indicated that the assessment was based on "currently available information" and "may change as additional information is collected and analyzed and current information continues to be evaluated."[60] Executive branch officials and members of Congress used the initial assessment to discuss the attack publicly. The revised assessment ultimately indicated that the attack "was a deliberate and organized terrorist attack carried out by extremists."[61] Analysis is an evolutionary process and can change over time as more information becomes available to create a clearer picture of the circumstances surrounding an event.[62]

The fight over the talking points occurred during the last several weeks of the presidential campaign race between President Obama and Republican contender Mitt Romney. Such a politically charged environment has always been a concern for the IC, as our interviewees indicated.[63] Although the interview participants stopped short of calling it "intentional bias," sending information out to a "hyper political external environment" meant that intelligence consumers "were far more likely to infer ill intent when something changed and they didn't understand why."[64] Following the Benghazi attacks and subsequent investigations by the Senate and House Select Committees, there was a perception that the IC had been burned by having its tentative assessments become a "political football" in the presidential campaign.[65] Ironically, press reporting on the conclusions of the House Select

---

[59] ODNI, "Statement by the Director of Public Affairs for ODNI, Shawn Turner, on the Intelligence Related to the Terrorist Attack on the U.S. Consulate in Benghazi, Libya," press release, September 28, 2012.

[60] ODNI, "Benghazi Emails on Unclassified Talking Points," May 29, 2013.

[61] ODNI, 2012.

[62] ODNI, 2012.

[63] Former senior officials, interviews with the authors.

[64] Former senior officials, interviews with the authors.

[65] David Ignatius, "CIA Documents Supported Susan Rice's Description of Benghazi Attacks," *Washington Post*, October 19, 2012.

Committee investigation was confusing. Although some outlets reported that the committee found that the IC committed no wrongdoing, others reported two years later that the committee found that CIA reports "were 'rife with errors'" and "misguided planning."[66]

The IC's concern with what analysts could say that was accurate, unclassified, and not likely "to impact any potential legal prosecution" and policymakers' need for immediate unclassified points to tell the media were two competing priorities.[67] The timeline, the hyper-partisan political climate and the sensitive nature of the event increased the possibility not only for bias to occur but also for the perception that something nefarious did occur. The revised intelligence assessment, the back-and-forth with the policymakers, and the CIA talking points being called "controversial" in the Senate Committee's report created the perception that the IC might not have been working objectively or independently.

Selective Declassification

President Obama's administration also used the practice of selective declassification to help the policy agenda. Sasha Dudding defined *selective declassification* as "the *authorized declassification*; of a *discrete set of material*; done to achieve *a self-serving political goal (beyond simply transparency)*; shared with a chosen *audience* (often the press); that results in an *intentionally misleading* impression of the topic."[68] Dudding called selective declassification "concerning" because it ultimately "harms the free flow of information by skewing our discussions and choices."[69]

---

[66] Ian Tuttle, "House Intel Investigation on Benghazi Clears Administration, Intelligence Community of Wrongdoing," *National Review*, November 21, 2014; Mary Troyan, "House Benghazi Committee Files Final Report and Shuts Down," *USA Today*, December 12, 2016.

[67] Policymaker, interview with the authors; ODNI, 2013.

[68] Sasha Dudding, "Spinning Secrets: The Dangers of Selective Declassification," *Yale Law Journal*, Vol. 130, No. 3, January 2021, p. 715.

[69] Dudding, 2021, p. 708.

For years, intelligence experts have been warning of the dangers of taking intelligence out of context.[70] These warnings sounded during Obama's presidency as well, as experts "cautioned against drawing broad conclusions about the state of Al Qaeda and Bin Laden's role in the organization" based on the declassified selection of documents collected during the raid on bin Laden's compound in Abbottabad, Pakistan, on May 1, 2011.[71] Although the administration publicly announced that its intent behind the declassification was to be more transparent by responding to the "increasing public demand to review those documents," the declassified documents seemed to raise more questions than they answered.[72] For example, questions abounded regarding why no photographic or other evidence of Osama bin Laden's death had been released.[73] The documents also provided an inconsistent narrative about the state of bin Laden and al Qaeda around the time of the raid.

Some of the documents that were declassified and released in 2012 in time for the anniversary of the raid suggested that bin Laden was weak at the time of the raid and that his terrorist organization "was under a great deal of stress" and "had been diminished.[74] In 2012, President Obama was running for reelection against presidential candidate Romney in a negative political climate after the terrorist attacks in Benghazi. Public polls from the previous year indicated that just more than half of the polled registered voters (56 percent in a CBS News and *New York Times* poll and 58 percent in a Fox News poll) approved of the job the President was doing on the issue of terrorism.[75] According to a different Fox News poll, 65 percent of the

---

[70] See, for example, "'Intelligence Matters' Host Michael Morell on the Top Global Threats in 2022," CBS News, updated January 6, 2022.

[71] Matthew Rosenberg, "In Osama Bin Laden Library: Illuminati and Bob Woodward," *New York Times*, May 20, 2015.

[72] Rosenberg, 2015.

[73] Office of the Press Secretary, "Press Briefing by Press Secretary Jay Carney, 5/4/2011," Washington, D.C.: Obama White House Archives, May 4, 2011.

[74] Office of the Press Secretary, "Press Briefing by Press Secretary Jay Carney, 5/3/12," Washington, D.C.: Obama White House Archives, May 3, 2012.

[75] Here, we are referring to the results of one specific question in each poll. In the CBS and *New York Times* poll, we looked at question 4, "Do you approve or disapprove of the

respondents felt that "Congress should continue to investigate the Obama administration's handling of the (September 2012) terrorist attack on the U.S. consulate in Benghazi, Libya, that resulted in the deaths of four Americans until lawmakers feel they know the truth."[76] The 2012 release affirmed to the voters that the Obama administration was successfully combating terrorism and was a positive message for the President's reelection campaign.

Contrary to the 2012 release, some of the documents released in 2015 showed that bin Laden continued to control al Qaeda and was therefore still a critical target.[77] In 2015, Seymour M. Hersh published a news article claiming that the raid was staged, and the Obama administration had lied about it.[78] The different conclusions drawn from the information provided to the public in 2015 and the separate document releases, coupled with the timing of the 2015 release, created the perception that the Obama administration was responding to Hersh's article.[79]

Additionally, the bin Laden raid boosted President Obama's chances for reelection and raised significant questions. The IC ultimately released nearly 485 gigabytes of files (about 500,000 files) from the raid. The raid yielded nearly 2.7 terabytes of files, for a release of approximately 0.04 per-

---

way Barack Obama is handling the threat of terrorism?" In the Fox News poll, we looked at question 11, "Do you approve or disapprove of the job Barack Obama is doing on the following issues? . . . Terrorism" (CBS News and *New York Times*, "Poll: Obama and the Republicans in Congress/Gun Control/Syria," version 2, data set, Ithaca, N.Y.: Cornell University, Roper Center for Public Opinion Research, 2013; Fox News, "Poll: Obama/ Sarah Palin/Economy/Osama bin Laden: August 2011," version 2, data set, Ithaca, N.Y.: Cornell University, Roper Center for Public Opinion Research, August 2011).

[76] Here, we are referring to the results of question 34, "Do you think Congress should continue to investigate the Obama administration's handling of the (September 2012) terrorist attack on the US consulate in Benghazi, Libya that resulted in the deaths of four Americans until lawmakers feel they know the truth, or not?" (Fox News, "Poll: Obama/ Health Care/Privacy," version 2, data set, Ithaca, N.Y.: Cornell University, Roper Center for Public Opinion Research, November 2013.

[77] ODNI, "Bin Laden's Bookshelf," webpage, undated a; Dudding, 2021, p. 741.

[78] Rosenberg, 2015.

[79] Dudding, 2021, pp. 739–740.

cent of the total files gathered.[80] The declassified files did not appear to pack much political ammunition. However, the decision to selectively declassify files from the mission that killed the U.S.'s most-wanted terrorist appeared to be more effective. A Gallup poll showed that the President's job approval rating from May 20, 2015 (the date of the release of the first batch of files) to the time he left office increased from 46 percent to 56 percent.[81]

Conclusion

In this chapter, we outlined evidence from the literature, reports, news articles, and interviews that the IC experienced some challenges with external bias during Obama's presidency and grappled with tension among the policymakers it supported. Earlier, we discussed how our interview participants observed a misalignment of incentives between the IC and policymakers. We found that a misalignment existed among the policymakers in the executive and legislative branches, along with examples of selective declassification. Philip Tetlock and Barbara Mellers have dubbed these the "clashing elites (to whom the IC must answer)."[82]

We also found that there is an internal struggle within the IC. The IC tries to maintain its independence while trying to fulfill its obligation to the customers it supports. Tetlock and Mellers have also observed this trade-off "between the clashing institutional-design goals of responsiveness and independence," where *responsiveness* means that the IC has to answer all legitimate requests of elected officials and *independence* requires insulation of the IC from policymakers.[83] We discuss this tension in greater detail in the conclusion of this report. Both responsiveness and independence led to problems for the IC during Obama's presidency. Our interviews also

---

[80] Emily Rand, "Source: 2.7 Terabytes of Data Recovered from Bin Laden Compound," CBS News, May 6, 2011.

[81] Gallup, "Gallup Daily: Obama Job Approval," webpage, undated.

[82] Philip E. Tetlock and Barbara A. Mellers, "Intelligent Management of Intelligence Agencies: Beyond Accountability Ping-Pong," *American Psychologist*, Vol. 66, No. 6, 2011, p. 542.

[83] Tetlock and Mellers, 2011, p. 543.

revealed the tension between IC independence and service to different customers and noted that the solution on avoiding inherent biases must come from the IC and its analysts. The policymaker ultimately wants to get out of the IC analyst what they need to support decisionmaking or the creation of policy.

Overall, several of our interview participants indicated that more-sophisticated intelligence consumers had a better relationship with the IC. These policymakers made "clear conscious efforts to avoid communications with the IC to skew results" or to influence them to produce particular assessments, while policymakers who were less familiar with the IC were not as able "to absorb conclusions at face value."[84] On the other hand, the policymakers who understood the IC better were also more cognizant of how to ask questions of the IC, which mattered for the product that these policymakers wanted to get. These intelligence consumers needed to be specific about what they wanted in order to get the right product for policy deliberations. Supporting policymaking is a delicate business because external pressure from Congress, the public, and policymakers to deliver an answer in favor of a policy or an administration position "[is] almost always" there.[85] But this pressure did not affect how the IC answered questions. The IC used judgment that could withstand analytical rigor to answer those questions.

---

[84] Former senior official, interview with the authors.

[85] Former senior official, interview with the authors.

CHAPTER EIGHT

The Trump Administration (2017–2021)

Whereas the study team had the benefit of numerous historical accounts and official document releases after the previously reviewed administrations ended, the Trump administration ended only one year prior to the writing of this report. Therefore, official document releases have been more limited. However, news reporting related to President Trump's contentious relationship with the IC throughout his administration was abundant. President Trump himself tried to deflect some of these reports, particularly with an address he gave at the CIA on January 21, 2017 (his first full day in office), in which he said,

> [T]he reason you're my first stop is that, as you know, I have a running war with the media. . . . And they sort of made it sound like I had a feud with the intelligence community. And I just want to let you know, the reason you're the number-one stop is exactly the opposite.[1]

However, Trump's campaign and first days in office also contained a good deal of criticism of the agencies he directed. Indeed, President Trump had tweeted less than three weeks before, "The 'Intelligence' briefing on so-called 'Russian hacking' was delayed until Friday, perhaps more time needed to build a case. Very strange!"[2] Over the next four years, President

---

[1] "Trump CIA Speech Transcript," CBS News, January 23, 2017.

[2] Jeremy Diamond, Evan Perez, Pamela Brown, and Jim Sciutto, "Trump Derides Intel Briefing on 'So-Called' Russian Hacking," CNN, January 4, 2017; Hasani Gittens and Ken Dilanian, "Trump Takes Jab at 'Intelligence' Officials for Allegedly Delaying 'Rus-

Trump's deeply contentious relationship with the IC continued to unfold in his tweets and in media reporting. During his time in office, there were two directors of the CIA; six secretaries of Homeland Security; and five Directors of National Intelligence (DNIs).[3] Moreover, the President's tweets about the IC did not stop. On January 30, 2019, President Trump tweeted,

> The Intelligence people seem to be extremely passive and naïve when it comes to the dangers of Iran. They are wrong! When I became President Iran was making trouble all over the Middle East, and beyond. Since ending the terrible Iran Nuclear Deal, they are MUCH different, but . . . a source of potential danger and conflict. . . . Be careful of Iran. Perhaps Intelligence should go back to school![4]

Through his time in office, President Trump and other administration officials consistently sought to influence—and, in some cases, bias—intelligence. What made the Trump administration notable was the introduction of bias with the intent of overtly achieving domestic political priorities. Interviews with former policymakers and senior IC officials reveal this trend. Interviewees discussed biased intelligence with regard to Russian interference in the 2016 and 2020 elections, immigration in support of harsher border security, the travel ban, white supremacists and antifa, refugees, the SolarWinds hack, domestic terrorism, mass shootings, and the coronavirus disease 2019 (COVID-19) pandemic.[5] In this chapter, we discuss the primary ways in which this bias emerged: by putting policy officials in charge of intelligence estimates, pressuring intelligence officials until

---

sian Hacking' Briefing," NBC News, January 4, 2017; John Wagner and Greg Miller, "Trump Alleges Delay in His Briefing on 'So-Called' Russian Hacking; U.S. Official Says There Wasn't One," *Washington Post*, January 4, 2017.

[3] Mike Pompeo and Gina Haspel served as CIA directors; U.S. Department of Homeland Security secretaries were John Kelly, Elaine Duke, Kirstjen Nelson, Kevin McAleenan, Chad Wolf, and Peter Gaynor; and Mike Dempsey, Dan Coats, Joseph Maguire, Richard Grenell, and John Ratcliffe served as DNIs.

[4] Olivia Beavers, "Trump Blasts Intel Chiefs as 'Passive and Naïve,'" *The Hill*, January 30, 2019.

[5] Former senior officials, interviews with the authors.

they backed down, and putting just enough "truthiness" in public statements to avoid being contradicted.

Policy Officials in Charge of Intelligence

Throughout his four years in office, President Trump consistently appointed policy-affiliated individuals to head portions of the IC. Furthermore, many of these individuals did not have adequate intelligence experience to hold the positions to which they were appointed. This is perhaps most readily seen in the appointment of John Ratcliffe as DNI. The Senate confirmed Ratcliffe to the post in May 2020, but that was not the first time President Trump had tried to install him as DNI. Trump withdrew Ratcliffe's first nomination in August 2019 after several Republican senators raised questions about the Texas congressman. Senate Intelligence Committee Chairman Richard Burr, Republican of North Carolina, said, "I don't know John Ratcliffe. . . . I talked to him on the phone last night—it's the first contact I've ever had with him. I look forward to getting to know him, and if I get an official nomination, I'll process it through the committee." Senator Susan Collins, Republican of Maine, indicated that the position should be filled by someone "with the integrity and skill and ability to bring all the members of the intelligence community together." Meanwhile, Senator Marco Rubio, Republican of Florida, said that the DNI needs "to make sure that the entire intelligence community is working in an apolitical way to arrive at a set of facts that policymakers can make decisions on." Rubio also said, "I wouldn't say that I'm concerned that [Ratcliffe is] incapable of doing that job. I certainly think that's going to be an issue among Democrats and others that we're going to have to confront, because I do think the D.N.I. needs to be someone that goes in with a strong vote of support."[6]

Throughout the confirmation processes in 2019 and 2020, both Democrats and IC professionals raised concerns that Ratcliffe would act as a political partisan in a position designed to be apolitical. Senator Ron Wyden,

---

[6] All senators are quoted in Julian E. Barnes, Nicholas Fandos, and Adam Goldman, "Republican Senators Are Cool to Trump's Choice for Top Intelligence Post," *New York Times*, July 29, 2019.

Democratic of Oregon, said, "Congressman Ratcliffe is the most partisan and least qualified individual ever nominated to serve as director of national intelligence." According to Wyden, Ratcliffe's only qualification was "his record of promoting Donald Trump's conspiracy theories." David Laufman, a former Justice Department official, said, "Mr. Ratcliffe's partisan political behavior on behalf of the president, including attacks on the special counsel's investigation, raises serious questions about whether he possesses the requisite qualities to fulfill that responsibility."[7]

Others raised concerns that Ratcliffe did not have the requisite experience for the position. According to 50 U.S. Code § 3023, "Any individual nominated for appointment as Director of National Intelligence shall have extensive national security expertise." Many raised concerns that Ratcliffe did not have such a background. The Texas congressman was initially elected in 2014.[8] Prior to his election to Congress, he was mayor of Heath, Texas, from 2004 to 2012, during which time he spent four years as a federal prosecutor.[9] By comparison, the first DNI, John Negroponte, was a foreign service officer, former NSC staffer, and four-time ambassador; he also had spent four years as the ambassador to the United Nations and as U.S. envoy to Iraq after the 2003 invasion. The next, Mike McConnell, served for 30 years in naval intelligence, was head of intelligence for the Joint Chiefs of Staff during Operation Desert Storm and was the chief of the NSA. Dennis Blair also spent his career in national security, including years as head of Pacific Command and as an associate director of the CIA. The longest-serving DNI, James Clapper, spent 40 years in intelligence: as a career Air Force intelligence officer, chief of DIA and the National Geospatial Intelligence Agency, and Under Secretary of Defense for Intelligence. Even President Trump's first choice for the role, former Senator Dan Coats, had spent 25 years in Congress, including on the Senate Intelligence Committee, and

---

[7] Barnes, Fandos, and Goldman, 2019.

[8] While a congressman, Ratcliffe served on the Homeland Security Committee from 2015 to 2019 and on the Intelligence Committee in the 116th Congress.

[9] Ken Dilanian, "Intel Officials Worry Trump's Pick for Top Spy Will Politicize the Job," NBC News, July 29, 2019.

four years as ambassador to Germany.[10] All told, Ratcliffe was confirmed to the post by a 49–44 vote and was the first DNI to be installed on a party-line vote.[11]

Ratcliffe was not the only policy-oriented official to be appointed to an intelligence post. Mike Pompeo, before becoming Secretary of State, served as director of the CIA. Also a former congressman, Pompeo rose to prominence criticizing the Obama administration's approach to the Iran nuclear deal and handling of the Benghazi attacks.[12] Acting DNI Richard Grenell, before serving as ambassador to Germany, had been the spokesman for four U.S. ambassadors during the Bush administration and for several Republican elected officials. One of Grenell's first hires was Kashyap Patel, who was best known as the "lead author of a politically charged memo . . . that accused F.B.I. and Justice Department leaders of abusing their surveillance powers to spy on a former Trump campaign adviser."[13] Grenell and Patel purged ODNI of established and respected figures, including Joseph Maguire and Andrew Hallman.

In interviews with former IC officials, they discussed the effect these appointments had on the estimative process. One former IC senior official said,

> [i]t is hard for me as an American taxpayer to watch policymakers talk about avoiding politicization and [still staff] senior posts in the IC with political appointees. . . . For instance, the Senior Director of the NSC, in the last two administrations, they had Hill staffers. If you have someone from a Congressional career and office in those kinds of positions, don't be surprised if you get political results."[14]

---

[10] Backgrounds of the DNIs are outlined in Garrett M. Graff, "Trump's New Intelligence Chief Spells Trouble," *Wired*, May 26, 2020.

[11] Mary Clare Jalonick and Eric Tucker, "Divided Senate Confirms Ratcliffe as Intelligence Chief," AP News, May 21, 2020.

[12] Barnes, Fandos, and Goldman, 2019.

[13] Julian E. Barnes, Adam Goldman, and Nicholas Fandos, "Richard Grenell Begins Overhauling Intelligence Office, Prompting Fears of Partisanship," *New York Times*, February 21, 2020.

[14] Former senior IC leader, interview with the authors.

These political results included Ratcliffe declassifying unverified intelligence reports on Hillary Clinton, intelligence that CIA director Gina Haspel said should remain secret. Marc Polymeropoulos, the former head of the CIA's clandestine operations in Europe and Russia, said, "We have never seen a senior intelligence official so politicized as Ratcliffe. . . . When the head of the C.I.A. pleads to not disclose information, it is extraordinary that he wanted to push forward."[15] Polymeropoulos would go on to say,

> What we are seeing here is the worst-case scenario that was raised by the Democrats during Ratcliffe's confirmation of putting such a political loyalist and national security neophyte into this important position. . . . He is cherry-picking intelligence, and seriously risks exposing sources and methods for absolutely no reason other than to promote and protect the president before the election.[16]

Reports also indicated that additional releases were aimed at "discrediting the Obama administration and trying to undercut the intelligence community assessment that showed Russia favored Mr. Trump and worked to help him get elected in 2016."[17] In sum, putting policy officials in charge of intelligence led to concerns about partisanship and biased intelligence, concerns that were most starkly felt by IC professionals. Next, we discuss how those professionals reacted to bias and partisanship.

Intelligence Officials with No Incentive to Dissent

The IC has always faced an inherent tension in its mission: having to provide customers with political interests independent, nonpartisan intelligence. The incentives for the IC are to receive positive feedback on the information presented; there are no benefits to receiving negative feedback. One inter-

---

[15] Quoted in Julian E. Barnes and Adam Goldman, "John Ratcliffe Pledged to Stay Apolitical. Then He Began Serving Trump's Political Agenda," *New York Times*, October 9, 2020.

[16] Quoted in Shane Harris, "DNI Ratcliffe Has Broken His Promise to Keep Politics out of Intelligence, Intelligence Veterans Say," *Washington Post*, October 8, 2020.

[17] Barnes and Goldman, 2020.

viewee said, "The IC was more insulated because of institutional culture [but] action doesn't translate into incentive structure. There is no structure where the IC gets rewarded for speaking truth to power."[18] However, this leads to a situation in which IC officials will withdraw—not provide dissenting analyses—to avoid raising the ire of policy officials. This occurred frequently during the Trump administration. An interview with a former IC official and policymaker reflected how the "culture of fear was real. People felt like they couldn't speak up even though they are THE national security person in the room."[19] The interviewee went on to say, "The IC gets tired of being bullied, then they withdraw."[20] Another interviewee said, "The IC's deeper feeling is that alternative viewpoints were not welcome. People were afraid in meetings. Certain people could tell the Administration that their ideas were bad, but they wouldn't get invited back to meetings because they held their ground."[21]

Besides not being invited back to meetings, IC officials faced the possibility of greater repercussions if they pushed back too far against the policy line. One interviewee said,

> [t]he morale has gone down in the IC. . . . In normal situations, the IC person will be pretty vocal about the intelligence. I saw this happen repeatedly that staying quiet was the best option because speaking out means being fired or an onslaught of pushback by the more political agencies in the room or by politicians.[22]

Political agencies and politicians frequently said that the intelligence representative was a part of the "deep state" if they dissented from the policy line. According to an interviewee, politicians can discredit "what the IC is saying. It happens with the national security community and the IC, putting out products and people saying it's biased or the deep state because it's

---

[18] Former senior policymaker, interview with the authors.

[19] Former senior policymaker, interview with the authors.

[20] Former senior policymaker, interview with the authors.

[21] Former senior policymaker, interview with the authors.

[22] Former senior policymaker, interview with the authors.

not what they want to hear."[23] Another individual said, "It's unfortunate to see this happening after an administration that was running down the IC saying that the IC was part of the deep state."[24]

In his book, Chris Whipple described how CIA director Gina Haspel acceded to White House pressure and did not disagree with the policy line after the assassination of journalist Jamal Khashoggi. The difference between the policy officials and the IC centered on the role of Saudi Arabian crown prince Mohammad bin Salman in the assassination. In November 2018, the IC concluded with "high confidence" that bin Salman was directly involved in the planning and execution of the murder. President Trump, however, discredited that assessment. In a written statement, President Trump said,

> After my heavily negotiated trip to Saudi Arabia last year, the Kingdom agreed to spend and invest $450 billion in the United States. . . . Our intelligence agencies continue to assess all information, but it could very well be that the Crown Prince had knowledge of this tragic event—maybe he did and maybe he didn't![25]

In its report on the killing, the CIA had concluded that bin Salman was involved on the basis of 11 messages exchanged between the assassins and the Saudi palace and phone intercepts between the leader of the murder team and bin Salman's office. Furthermore, Whipple quotes an intelligence official who said, "I've been told that at least some body parts went back to Riyadh, to the crown prince."[26] Haspel had an opportunity to push back on President Trump's equivocation at a congressional hearing on November 28, 2018, prior to a vote on aid to Saudi Arabia. Secretary of State Mike Pompeo and Secretary of Defense James Mattis appeared for the closed-door hearing. Haspel did not. Whipple wrote that "Haspel had failed a major test: Asked to testify to Congress about a matter of national importance and international interest, she'd caved to White House pressure and stayed away." According

---

[23] Former senior policymaker, interview with the authors.

[24] Former senior IC leader, interview with the authors.

[25] As quoted in Whipple, 2020, pp. 310–311.

[26] Whipple, 2020, p. 311.

to Whipple, "It was Pompeo who reportedly told Haspel to stay away from Capitol Hill."[27]

In addition to the Khashoggi episode, interviewees discussed situations in which the IC did not dissent despite the administration's biased use of intelligence. The two most prominent scenarios involved any suggestions of Russian meddling in elections and white supremacy. With regard to Russia, one former policymaker said, "With election interference, there were attempts to directly impact/change what the intelligence said. The IC was going to say that Russia did something, but policymakers would also insist on adding more language, like something else about Iran."[28] A former IC senior official said, "In the situation supporting election security, which is the third rail of intelligence topics, we had folks who were participating in some of the legislatively mandated estimates on foreign interference and it was an awkward process."[29] Another former intelligence official said, "There was all of the coverage around Russia meddling in the election. The Administration didn't understand our core values or mission so they assumed we were a political actor. It's hard to argue against that."[30] Interviewees also mentioned the degree to which the administration biased intelligence by tasking assignments in certain ways. One policymaker said, "In the Trump Administration it was a one-sided narrative. Certain topics went untouched—like white supremacy. There were external pressures wanting [the Department of Homeland Security] to leave out the far-right threat and white supremacy and to only focus on Antifa."[31] With no structural incentives to provide dissenting views on the topic, and facing political risks for dissent, the IC throughout the Trump era would withdraw and stay quiet. This allowed policy officials to freely use biased intelligence or cherry-pick intelligence to suit the administration's line.

---

[27] Whipple, 2020, p. 311.

[28] Former senior policymaker, interview with the authors.

[29] Former senior IC leader, interview with the authors.

[30] Former senior IC leader, interview with the authors.

[31] Former senior policymaker, interview with the authors.

Just Enough "Truthiness" in Talking Points

Similar to the Bush administration's use of biased intelligence to sell the American public on the Iraq War, the Trump administration would take cherry-picked intelligence to score domestic political points. Talking points were the format in which this process became most obvious. Interviewees highlighted how administration officials would get just enough "truthiness" in talking points. Other methods of using intelligence in a biased manner included trying to get the IC to disprove a negative or politicizing information that is not present.

One former policymaker highlighted these factors in particularly stark terms, saying,

> [d]uring the Trump Administration, in battles between the IC and the Administration, the IC would not change its finding, but policy-makers would add an amendment, something the IC couldn't disprove. . . . Administration representatives learned from their mistakes when dealing with the IC and would get enough 'truthiness' in talking points they wanted.[32]

This policymaker specifically cited immigration and the border as situations in which this dynamic emerged. A different former policymaker confirmed these conclusions:

> There was definitely some external pressure on pushing the narrative on what migrant caravans were or were not—a bunch of terrorists ready to infiltrate or people fleeing persecution or poor people trying to find a better life. Maybe this happens every year and we just have a closer eye on it now.[33]

The intelligence around the migrants highlights how the administration could ask the IC to prove a negative by asking, "Can you prove that the migrants are not terrorists?" Because evidence could prove only whether there were terrorists present, IC officials were left in a quandary: They could

---

[32] Former senior policymaker, interview with the authors.

[33] Former senior policymaker, interview with the authors.

not prove that terrorists were not a part of the caravans even if they had seen nothing to indicate the presence of such individuals.

The Trump administration would spin intelligence in talking points by referring obliquely to "what the IC said." One policymaker said that the administration would selectively declassify information to support certain narratives, thereby

> manipulating the information to be released and using the IC as the cover for it and taking it out of context—saying, "the IC said this." It was classic for the administration to do that. It puts a lot of people in really bad situations. They tried to do that with Ukraine and Russia and election security.[34]

Such trends were especially noticeable with election interference, in which conflating the actions of Russia and China became a central flashpoint. The same policymaker said, "They conflated that and ran with it. That's how the acting DNI got pushed out."[35]

A policymaker also related an instance in which administration officials worked to politicize information that was not there. This interviewee said,

> You see a sort of bullying in the NSC in the Africa Directorate. . . . [An Africa expert] was looking at the persecution of Christians because that hits the evangelical part and that hits the Vice President because he is Christian, and she is trying to politicize stuff that isn't there. A lot of Agency analysts in the Africa Directorate left. They actually were asked to be pulled back because they wouldn't tell her what she wants to hear.[36]

More specifically, the policymaker highlighted atrocities in Nigeria. The interviewee said,

> [w]ith Nigeria and the persecution of Christians, I had a conversation with the [Vice President's] Chief of Staff. He said it's a genocide

---

[34] Former senior policymaker, interview with the authors.

[35] Former senior policymaker, interview with the authors.

[36] Former senior policymaker, interview with the authors.

of Christians. I said no, it's killing a lot of people, not just Christians. The IC would say it's persecution across the board. The reason they are going after this is not to go after Boko Haram. It's to say that we are protecting Christians.[37]

Conclusion

Putting policy officials in charge of intelligence, intelligence officials having no incentive to dissent, and policymakers getting just enough "truthiness" in talking points all occurred during the Trump administration. Thus far, we have discussed how biased intelligence estimates emerged under many Presidents, both Democratic and Republican. However, the degree to which the Trump administration biased intelligence, and its reason for doing so, bears special mention. In previous chapters, we highlighted specific episodes or individuals who put their thumbs on the scale with regard to intelligence estimates. Under President Trump, the distortion of intelligence and truth seems to have risen to new heights. Interviewees mentioned biased intelligence about Russia, China, Iran, Ukraine, Africa, counterterrorism, election interference, immigration, border security, the travel ban, white supremacy, domestic terrorism, antifa, refugees, the COVID-19 pandemic, mass shootings, and a variety of other homeland security–related endeavors. The sheer variety and scope of topics covered dwarf those in any other administration. Moreover, Trump administration officials were much more blatant about what they were doing when introducing bias. Calling dissenters "part of the deep state," firing uncooperative intelligence officials, and not inviting intelligence professionals to meetings all worked to ensure that Trump policymakers enacted their chosen policies regardless of whether the intelligence supported the decision. Distorting the intelligence to support domestic political priorities (especially election interference and migrant issues) became quotidian. Putting such individuals as John Ratcliffe, Mike Pompeo, and Ric Grenell in charge of intelligence estimates likely contributed to a biased lens. Since the formation of the IC in 1947, no other administration has used and abused intelligence to the same degree or with the same motives.

---

[37] Former senior policymaker, interview with the authors.

CHAPTER NINE

Conclusions and Looking Forward

After reviewing the history of perceived bias in intelligence estimates since the start of the Cold War, we arrived at several conclusions. First, the degree of perceived bias in intelligence estimates is highly dependent on the presidential administration in power. Second, the most common reason for bias from policymakers is the desire to minimize the appearance of dissent. Third, the most common reason for bias internal to the IC is self-censorship: The IC is either trying to maintain its relevance and utility or avoiding the ire of policymakers. Finally, there appears to be an inherent tension in the IC-policymaker relationship: The IC has an incentive to elicit positive feedback. There are no benefits, either to careers or budgets, for negative feedback. This creates friction between the mission of providing policymakers objective information and serving the policymakers as customers. In this chapter, we discuss each of these conclusions in more depth.

Bias Is Dependent on Presidential Administration

The first and foremost conclusion we were able to draw is that the degree of bias in intelligence estimates greatly depends on the presidential administration in power. Some administrations bias and politicize intelligence less, some more. Moreover, each President has a different relationship with the IC. Especially during the early years, intelligence officials played a crucial role in the policymaking process. Such DCIs as Allen Dulles and John McCone were heavily involved in planning Cold War policy under President Kennedy. However, not all Presidents had such a relationship with their DCIs. Under President Clinton, White House staff secretary John Podesta recalled what the President thought of DCI Woolsey. Podesta said that they were "oil and water" and "Clinton just did not like the guy." After one meet-ing, Podesta recalled that Clinton said, "I don't ever want to see that man again."[1] What these differing relationships show is the spectrum of how Presidents will need and treat information. Some Presidents who rely heav-ily on intelligence to make and sell their foreign policy decisions might need to bias estimates to minimize the appearance of dissent or gloss over poten-tially negative repercussions. Presidents who exclude intelligence from the policymaking process and do not rely on the IC have much less of a need to bias estimates. There are no constitutional requirements that the Presi-dent actually read and consider the products of the IC, so those who wish to ignore the information are free to do so.

The administration in power is also the primary driver of both external and internal bias. The IC is part of the Executive Branch, and it has pri-marily been other Executive Branch officials seeking to introduce bias into intelligence. Whether it is Walt Rostow saying, "I'm sorry you won't sup-port your president," to a CIA analyst dissenting from the Vietnam O/B fig-ures or Douglas Feith standing up a quasi-intelligence unit in the Pentagon to produce more useful data in the lead-up to the Iraq War, the President selects and commands those who seek to introduce external bias. However, it is equally important to note that when the IC self-censors, it is doing so because of how the President governs. When the IC changes its estimates in an effort to maintain relevance or avoid blowback from other political figures, it is because the President has allowed such a condition to exist. When DCI Richard Helms acceded to pressure from the Nixon administra-tion on the SS-9 missile, he said it was out of a desire to maintain the agen-cy's position in the government. If Helms had not been concerned about the repercussions of dissent, he would have been empowered to keep the IC's conclusions the way they were. Similarly, when Trump-era intelligence officials discuss how analysts avoided linking Russia's desire to elect Presi-dent Trump and election interference out of fear of retaliation from other policymakers, it is the responsibility of the President. Each President has a different relationship with the IC, and the nature of that relationship is the primary driver of biased estimates.

---

[1] As quoted in Whipple, 2020, p. 155.

Minimizing the Appearance of Dissent

The relationship with the President notwithstanding, policymakers most commonly seek to introduce bias in intelligence estimates to reduce the appearance of dissent. During the Vietnam War, MACV and Johnson administration officials pressured the CIA to change its estimates over the O/B to continue the appearance of a successful war. General Creighton Abrams said that it was important to continue "projecting an image of success."[2] Nixon administration policymakers wanted to bolster their tough-on-security credentials by pursuing missile defense. To do so, they needed to ensure that the CIA did not dissent with the policy line on the capabilities and intentions of the Soviet Union's SS-9 missile. Furthermore, George W. Bush–era policymakers consistently tried to use cherry-picked intelligence to make a better case for the Iraq War. The administration resisted any IC attempts to cast doubt on the links between Iraq and al Qaeda. Each of these situations, and many more, highlight the commonality in the motivation behind the introduction of external bias: Administration officials do not want to have to explain to the President, Congress, or the American people why a part of the executive branch disagrees with a chosen policy. In other words, policymakers want to reduce the appearance of any dissent.

Briefly consider what would have happened had the CIA's position prevailed on the Vietnamese O/B: General Westmoreland, National Security Adviser Rostow, Defense Secretary McNamara, Secretary of State Rusk, DCI Helms, and many others surely would have been called to testify before congressional committees and would have had to appear on the Sunday morning talk shows to answer uncomfortable questions, such as "Why is the U.S. effort in Vietnam not working?" "How long have U.S. efforts been in vain?" "Why should the United States continue its involvement in Southeast Asia?" "How can the United States be losing the war?" "Who is responsible?" and "If the United States cannot win in Vietnam, what happens if the Soviet Union advances through the Fulda Gap?" These questions would have been devastating for the Johnson administration, which was trying to minimize the war in Vietnam and advance the Great Society. Through this lens, it is clear why policymakers sought to bias intelligence that dissented from

---

[2]   Quoted in Ford, 1998, p. 85.

the policy line. Such motivations are present throughout the history of IC-policymaker relations. When the IC dissents, policymakers have to spend valuable time, energy, focus, and news cycles on questions and explanations about that dissent. It is much easier to avoid the appearance of disagreement in the first place.

Self-Censorship in the Intelligence Community

Of course, policymakers are not the only ones who introduce bias into intelligence estimates. The producers of those estimates are not immune from bias. Indeed, this is the entire point of having intelligence analysis tradecraft: to ensure that estimates are as objective and free from bias as possible. Such authors as Sherman Kent and Greg Treverton—and many others—have written about intelligence analysis standards. Despite these efforts, and the training that intelligence analysts must undergo, estimates still fall prey to bias. Jervis outlined some of these biases that occurred prior to the 1979 Islamic Revolution in Iran and the invasion of Iraq in 2003.[3] The most common internal bias we found was self-censorship, i.e., IC analysts and managers consciously changing or watering down assessments. This self-censorship was largely driven by one of two factors: a desire to stay relevant or an effort to avoid retaliation from policymakers. As noted earlier, DCI Richard Helms acceded to administration pressure at least twice in an effort to preserve the standing of the CIA. Interviewees also discussed the prevalence of self-censorship. One former IC senior official said,

> There was a risk averse, risk management attitude. . . . Our analysts had a concern that the desire to be deliberate could cause a bias. People were becoming so censored that they became biased. We were concerned that analysts would self-censor based on the risk aversion message.[4]

Intelligence agencies can be useful only if they can present information to policymakers. Intelligence officials also have career aspirations. Repeatedly

---

[3] Jervis, 2010a.

[4] Former IC senior leader, interview with the authors.

presenting unfavorable information to policymakers is detrimental to both of these objectives. As discussed in the chapter on the Trump administration, IC officials had no incentive to dissent from the policy line. Although the repercussions were particularly stark during the Trump era, the incentives are the same regardless of the presidential administration. When faced with possible retaliation or the simple desire to ensure the continuity of the IC's mission, self-censorship offers the IC an avenue of escape.

Tension in the Intelligence Community Mission

Finally, there is an inherent tension in the IC's mission. The IC, as a member of the executive branch, serves at the pleasure of the President. Nothing mandates the IC to produce unbiased intelligence, and there is no recourse short of congressional action to sanction improper use of intelligence. Moreover, there is nothing that requires the President to consider—much less act on—the best intelligence available. Politicians, not the IC, set policy, and there are no repercussions for policymakers who disregard intelligence. This creates a system in which the IC needs to cater to the administration's line to maintain its relevance (and, perhaps more importantly, its budget). An interview with one former policymaker highlights this tension. The interviewee said, "the incentives for the IC are based around positive feedback on the information they provide, there are no incentives to receive negative feedback. There is a tension between independence in the IC and serving customer number one. This has always been perplexing."[5]

Inscribed on a wall in CIA headquarters is the phrase "And Ye Shall Know the Truth and the Truth Shall Make You Free." The ODNI's *Principles of Professional Ethics for the Intelligence Community* state, "We seek the truth; speak truth to power; and obtain, analyze, and provide intelligence objectively."[6] In a CNN interview, CIA director Leon Panetta said

---

[5] Former senior policymaker, interview with the authors.

[6] ODNI, "Principles of Professional Ethics for the Intelligence Community," webpage, undated c.

that the job of the IC is to speak truth to power.[7] But what happens when the powers that be do not want the truth? The President has the power to appoint the CIA director, the FBI director, the head of the NSA, the DNI, and every other position of power within the IC. The President also has the ability to remove those individuals (even if it breaks conventional norms to do so). It is the mission of those in the IC to provide objective and unbiased estimates. However, as we have seen throughout this study, that does not always happen; part of the reason is because of the structure of the U.S. policymaker–intelligence system, which creates a tension between providing that intelligence and serving the needs of the customer.

Looking Forward

So, what is to be done with these conclusions? First, it is important to recognize that bias will never fully be eliminated from intelligence estimates. Many analyses are the result of long processes conducted by people who have their own interests and interpretations. This means that assessments in which people are involved will never be fully immune from psychological biases. Second, intelligence estimates can be wrong even when bias is not present. Analysts work in environments of deep uncertainty. They draw conclusions from incomplete information. It is possible, and indeed probable, that mistakes will be made at some point in time. With proper analytic tradecraft standards, intelligence failures can be minimized, but it is not practical to expect that they can be avoided forever. In 1978, Richard Betts wrote, "Observers who see notorious intelligence failures as egregious often infer that disasters can be avoided by perfecting norms and procedures for analysis and argumentation. This belief is illusory. . . . Intelligence failures are not only inevitable, they are natural."[8] Therefore, policymakers and the American public writ large must have realistic standards for what intelligence can and cannot do. Finally, much of the preceding analysis has discussed the role of policymakers in creating biased estimates. However, we

---

[7] "Panetta: Job of Intel Community Is to Speak Truth to Power," CNN, video, January 31, 2019.

[8] Betts, 1978, pp. 61, 88.

also recognize that policymakers have a right to, and indeed should, push back on intelligence estimates. The IC and its analysts are not always correct; there are chances of groupthink, weak evidence being used to draw conclusions, and bureaucratic preferences being considered before all else. The pushback from decisionmakers does not always—and need not—constitute politicization and biased estimates.

Preventing Bias in the Future

Given the conclusions outlined in the previous section, we present three thoughts about ways to prevent biased estimates in the future. First, it is imperative that uniform standards establish what constitutes improper bias and what does not. Although the IC conducts training on the types of bias that can affect analyses, IC analytic standards discuss bias in only the most general way. As we mentioned earlier, policymakers have every right to refute the conclusions of the IC. This does not always involve the introduction of bias, but it very well might. The important delineation is what distinguishes proper behavior from improper behavior. The key factor is the motivation behind the refutation of IC conclusions. If the policymaker or dissenting members of the IC push back out of a sincere desire to obtain the truth, that is a laudable goal. Problems emerge when policymakers are not seeking the truth and are instead looking for information that conforms to preconceived beliefs. These biases are particularly pernicious when the policymakers are (or the IC itself is) looking to use intelligence for domestic policy purposes or to sway public opinion toward a particular foreign policy course. Consider the way the George W. Bush administration used intelligence prior to the invasion of Iraq in 2003, or how Trump administration officials sought to twist information about migrants and refugees. In the former case, policymakers were using intelligence in an attempt to sway public opinion in favor of the war. In the latter case, the administration was looking to motivate its base, demonstrating why domestic political priorities (such as building a border wall) should take priority. In neither instance was the motivation a desire to arrive at the truth of the matter. This would therefore constitute improper bias.

Discerning motivations, however, is notoriously difficult. How much repeated questioning is too much? What happens if policymakers give public statements that are not supported by intelligence? What is the recourse if policymakers stand up independent quasi-intelligence shops? This second consideration should focus on the role of IGs in investigating impropriety by both politicians and civil servants. President Trump famously removed five IGs within the span of six weeks: Michael Atkinson of the IC, Mitch Behm of the Department of Transportation, Glenn Fine of DoD, Christi Grimm of Health and Human Services, and Steve Linick of the Department of State.[9] IGs cannot be expected to adequately carry out their duties if they are fired during the course of proper and necessary investigations, especially if they are investigating the people who have the ability to fire them. In his memoir of the Vietnam O/B scenario, CIA analyst Sam Adams discussed the fundamental problem with the CIA IG. Adams wrote of his meeting with two IG investigators after raising a complaint. According to Adams, the investigators said, "[W]e've finished our investigation, and now it's in the hands of Mr. Stewart [the IG]. He'll write the final report." Adams wrote, "At that point, I asked the obvious questions: 'Who writes Mr. Stewart's fitness report?' . . . 'The executive director does. That's Colonel White,' said [one of the IG investigators]. 'And who writes Colonel White's?' 'Mr. Helms.' 'And who appointed Gordon Stewart Inspector General?' 'Mr. Helms.'"[10] IGs, who no doubt care a great deal about the truth and fairness, can also be said to be career-motivated individuals who are interested in a continuing paycheck and the prospect of future employment. To adequately investigate claims of improperly biased intelligence, IGs should be insulated from the command structure and should have the ability to institute real and enforceable punishments for those who commit offenses.

A final consideration moving forward is whether policy-oriented individuals should be allowed to hold management positions within the IC, or, perhaps more accurately, what qualifications the individuals should hold before ascending to senior positions within the IC. As the section on John

---

[9] Melissa Quinn, "The Internal Watchdogs Trump Has Fired or Replaced," CBS News, May 19, 2020.

[10] Sam Adams, *War of Numbers: An Intelligence Memoir*, South Royalton, Vt.: Steerforth Press, 1994, p. 159.

Ratcliffe as the DNI shows, there was extensive concern, both within the IC and in the media, that the former Texas congressman did not have the requisite experience and would simply act in the political interests of President Trump. Such speculation inherently raises concern about the objectivity of intelligence. However, there is a delicate balance that needs to be struck. Former (and future) policymakers can make very effective intelligence leaders. George H. W. Bush is a prime example of this. The future Vice President and President served the CIA during a tumultuous time, when morale at the agency was low, with the media and Congress looking for the slightest transgression to pounce. Despite not having intelligence credentials (having been the de facto ambassador to China, the ambassador to the United Nations, chairman of the Republican National Committee, and a two-term Texas congressman), Bush undoubtedly served as an effective DCI. Long-time CIA official Charles Allen said, "[Bush] found us at a dark hour when all you heard were these 'rogue elephant' charges. . . . He defended the ramparts carefully, thoughtfully. He achieved a great reconciliation with Congress, by constantly courting its leaders, talking about the greatness of the Central Intelligence Agency—its people, its mission."[11] Furthermore, career intelligence officials are not immune from charges of politicization or bias themselves. Consider the accusations leveled against Robert Gates during the first confirmation process over Iran-Contra and the questions over Gina Haspel's role in running a black operations site and destroying videotapes of interrogations.[12] In the final measure, it is the responsibility of the President and the Senate to ensure that the right individuals serve at the highest levels of the IC. As the example of the Trump administration shows, there is no guarantee that the President will select highly qualified individuals who are above reproach or that the Senate will serve as an effective gatekeeper in preventing inexperienced persons from ascending to high office. One potential solution is to strengthen the language of 50 U.S. Code § 3023 by laying out what kind of "extensive national security expertise" is needed to effectively manage the intelligence agencies of the United States. More clearly delineating the expectations for IC managers would give senators a

---

[11] As quoted in Whipple, 2020, p. 85.

[12] We do not discuss the veracity of these accusations, merely the fact that they were leveled.

stronger position in preventing unqualified individuals from receiving confirmation and could stop Presidents from appointing those without the requisite experience to such offices.

In sum, after recognizing that some degree of bias will always be present, intelligence failures can occur without bias, and policymakers can push back against IC assessments without introducing bias, we offer three conclusions about minimizing bias moving forward. Establishing uniform standards of what exactly constitutes improper bias could help manage expectations for both the IC and policymakers. Policymakers would know what tactics are allowed in confronting estimates, while the IC could lessen its concerns about inappropriate influence. IGs could be empowered to carry out more-effective investigations by being removed from the chain of command and by being given the ability to levy real and effective discipline for transgressions. Finally, a review of existing U.S. law could help ensure that prudent and qualified individuals serve as the highest-level intelligence officials.

Decisionmaker Interview Protocol

**Recruitment and Consent—Decisionmaker Interviewees
Examining the Estimative Processes of the Intelligence Community**

The RAND Corporation is conducting a study to explore if, and to what degree, trust in intelligence predictions and national estimates may have been degraded over time, and what internal and external factors may be drivers of any perceived or real bias, inequity, or change. The study was conceived by RAND and funded through an OSD-approved Research Support fund. We intend to explore if, and to what degree, trust in intelligence predictions and national estimates may vary over time. We will generate recommendations for exploring these potential changes and for mapping its causes, consequences, and historical genesis. One component of this study is to speak with former policymakers and decisionmakers who were regular consumers of national level intelligence produced from the estimative processes of the National Intelligence Council. From these discussions, we hope to get a sense of how much decision-makers knew about what goes into the estimative process as consumers of its products, what their perceptions were about the objectivity of the analysis they received, any instances where they suspected bias in the process from internal IC, external policymaking, or other factors.

This is the purpose for our discussion with you today—to have a factual discussion and learn any insights you might share from your professional experience in this area over the course of your career. We expect the discussion will take no more than 60 minutes. We will be holding this discussion at the UNCLASSIFIED level, but if we need to arrange for a separate classified component to the discussion, please let us know and we can make arrangements.

RAND will only use this information for research purposes. Your responses are not-for-attribution and your identity will not be connected to your responses in any way.

We appreciate and value your participation. If you are willing to participate in this study, please remain in the room. If there are any questions that you prefer not to answer or if you would prefer to cease your participation at any time, you should feel free to do so. If you have any questions about this study, please contact the project leaders:

Rich Girven
(703) 413-1100 x5925
rgirven@rand.org

Sina Beaghley
(310) 393-0411 x6653
beaghley@rand.org

If you have questions about your rights as a research participant or need to report a research-related injury or concern, you can contact RAND's Human Subjects Protection Committee toll-free at (866) 697-5620 or by emailing hspcinfo@rand.org. Thank you!

Initial Interview Protocol Questions

1. Can you tell us about your background, solely as a way to understand your involvement (as a decisionmaker/policymaker and consumer) with the estimative processes of the IC? How long were you in this position(s)?
   a. What was the nature of the majority of the analytic products you received? Were they from primarily a specific intelligence agency or from a broad set of IC elements?
   b. Were you a regular consumer of national intelligence estimates (NIEs), Sense of the Community Memoranda (SOCM) or Intelligence Community Assessment (ICA)?
2. Were you ever a requestor for a NIE on a particular topic, or a part of the process of requesting a NIE (e.g., at the White House) on a specific topic?
   a. Can you tell us more about this, at an UNCLASSIFIED level?

3. From your perspective as an intelligence consumer, did you ever perceive that there were any internal (IC Agency or IC writ large) biases or pressures on national level analysis to come to a certain conclusion?
   a. Were you ever aware of official complaints of internal bias?
   b. Other internal IC issues you may be aware of, or think might be relevant to this study?
   c. Why did you perceive that there may be bias in the national level analysis you received?

4. From your perspective as an intelligence consumer, did you ever perceive that there were any external (administration, Cabinet Department, Joint Staff, Congress, etc.) biases or pressures that affected analysis?
   a. Were you ever aware of official complaints of external bias?
   b. Were you aware of instances of dissenting views or opposition from organizations external to the IC on NIEs? What was the nature of these?
   c. Other external issues you think might be relevant to this study?

5. If not already discussed, were you ever aware of pressure from the White House staff, NSC, or President to alter or change national level analysis? Or from the head of another Department/Agency?
   a. Can you provide some details?
   b. Was the pressure direct or indirect?
   c. What was the outcome (was analysis altered in any way?)

6. From your perspective as an intelligence consumer, did you ever perceive that trust in intelligence predictions and national estimates may have been degraded, from feedback by other decision-makers or other sources? If so, can you give an example of what happened and why you perceived this was the case?

7. Based on your experiences, what are the drivers for public trust or distrust in the Intelligence Community today?
   a. How has this changed throughout your career?

8. Is there any question we should have asked but didn't?

9. Is there anyone else you would recommend we talk to who might have relevant insights to inform our study?

Intelligence Community Member Interview Protocol

Recruitment and Consent—IC Interviewees

Examining the Estimative Processes of the Intelligence Community

The RAND Corporation is conducting a study to explore if, and to what degree, trust in intelligence predictions and national estimates may have been degraded over time, and what internal and external factors may be drivers of any perceived or real bias, inequity, or change. The study was conceived by RAND and funded through an OSD-approved Research Support fund. We intend to explore if, and to what degree, trust in intelligence predictions and national estimates may vary over time. We will generate recommendations for exploring these potential changes and for mapping its causes, consequences, and historical genesis. One component of this study is to speak with former and current IC officials who have worked in and around the estimative processes of the National Intelligence Council to better understand the process, how it may have changed over time, and any internal or external factors that may weigh upon the final analytic outcomes of NIEs, SOCMs, ICAs, and their predecessor documents.

This is the purpose for our discussion with you today—to have a factual discussion and learn any insights you might share from your professional experience in this area over the course of your career. We expect the discussion will take no more than 60 minutes. We will be holding this discussion at the UNCLASSIFIED level, but if we need to arrange for a separate classified component to the discussion, please let us know and we can make arrangements.

RAND will only use this information for research purposes. Your responses are not-for-attribution and your identity will not be connected to your responses in any way.

We appreciate and value your participation. If you are willing to participate in this study, please remain in the room. If there any questions that you prefer not to answer or if you would prefer to cease your participation at any time, you should feel free to do so. If you have any questions about this study, please contact the project leaders:

Rich Girven
(703) 413-1100 x5925
rgirven@rand.org

Sina Beaghley
(310) 393-0411 x6653
beaghley@rand.org

If you have questions about your rights as a research participant or need to report a research-related injury or concern, you can contact RAND's Human Subjects Protection Committee toll-free at (866) 697-5620 or by emailing hspcinfo@rand.org.

Initial IC Interview Protocol Questions

1. Can you tell us about your background, solely as a way to understand your involvement (user, manager, analyst, overseer, etc.) with the estimative processes of the IC?
    a. If you were an analyst or analytic manager, what was the highest level of government at which you briefed your work? If you managed others, can you offer a few insights into the importance of some of the work you managed (managed the IC's drafting of a dozen NIEs, was principal manager on a White House requested NIE, etc.).
2. We are hoping to note changes in process by asking different interviewees how the process worked while they were involved. If you worked in or near the NIE estimative process, can you say a little bit about the process at the time and how it unfolded. How were principal drafters selected, how were agency positions and dissents handled, how was the estimate reviewed and approved, etc?

    a.   What was the timeframe for this process?

    b.   Were there any major process changes during your involvement?

    c.   Were there any organizational changes in or around the NIC during your involvement?

3.   From your perspective as a (manager/analyst/overseer/other) did you ever perceive that there were any internal (IC Agency or IC writ large) biases or pressures on national level analysis to come to a certain conclusion? Why did you have the perception that there may be biases in the national level analysis?

    a.   Were you ever aware of complaints of bias brought to the IC Ombudsman or AIS?

    b.   How often would you say that there were dissenting views or official agency "dissents" to an NIE?

    c.   Other internal IC issues you think might be relevant to this study?

4.   From your perspective as a (manager/analyst/overseer/other) did you ever perceive that there were any external (administration, Cabinet Department, Joint Staff, Congress, etc.) biases or pressures that affected analysis?

    a.   Were you ever aware of complaints of external bias brought to the IC Ombudsman or AIS?

    b.   How often would you say that there were dissenting views or opposition from organizations external to the IC on NIEs?

    c.   Other external issues you think might be relevant to this study?

5.   If not already discussed, were you ever aware of pressure from the White House staff, NSC, or President to alter or change national level analysis? Or from the head of another Department/Agency?

    a.   Can you provide some details?

    b.   Was the pressure direct or indirect?

    c.   What was the outcome (was analysis altered in any way?)

6.   From your perspective as a (manager/analyst/overseer/other) did you ever perceive that the trust in intelligence predictions and national estimates may have been degraded, from feedback by decision-makers or other sources? If so, can you give an example of what happened and why you perceived this was the case?'

7. Based on your experiences, what are the drivers for public trust or distrust in the Intelligence Community today?
    a. How has this changed throughout your career?
8. Is there any question we should have asked but didn't?
9. Is there anyone else you would recommend we talk to who might have relevant insights to inform our study?

Literature Search Strategy

In this appendix, we describe the details of our literature review. First, we describe our exploratory review, in which we used broad search terms to identify relevant articles. The purpose of this exploratory review was to define the scope of research on trust and the IC. Second, we describe the methods of our systematic literature review.

Exploratory Literature Review

In the exploratory literature review, we used the following 18 search terms on such databases as JSTOR, Google Scholar, and ProQuest, to identify 27 articles:

- [intelligence analysis] and [bias]
- [intelligence analysis] and [public trust]
- [partisanship] and [intelligence]
- [public confidence] and [intelligence community]
- [skepticism] and [intelligence community]
- [public opinion] and [intelligence]
- [public opinion] and [intelligence community]
- [attitudes] and [intelligence community]
- [public distrust] and [intelligence]
- [public trust of intelligence]
- [public trust of intelligence community]
- [intelligence] and [trust]
- [bias] and [estimative process]
- [intelligence] and [public opinion]

- [trust] and [intelligence community]
- [intelligence community] and [public opinion]
- [trust in the intelligence community]
- [trust in intelligence].

We identified four key themes from this research. The first theme concerns reforming the IC. Articles concerning reform discussed assessing the value of structured analytic techniques in the IC,[1] the issue of secrecy,[2] metrics for assessing the estimative accuracy and value of analytic products,[3] and systemic issues in the analytic community.[4] The second theme we identified was bias in the estimative process. Articles on this theme include one on politicization using a case study approach,[5] Intelligence Community Directive 203 addressing analytic standards,[6] an article on the psychology of intelligence analysis,[7] and an article on intelligence analysis tradecraft.[8] The third theme is scholarship on intelligence failures. These articles include the

---

[1] Stephen Artner, Richard S. Girven, and James B. Bruce, *Assessing the Value of Structured Analytic Techniques in the U.S. Intelligence Community*, Santa Monica, Calif.: RAND Corporation, RR-1408-OSD, 2016.

[2] James B. Bruce, Sina Beaghley, and W. George Jameson, *Secrecy in U.S. National Security: Why a Paradigm Shift Is Needed*, Santa Monica, Calif.: RAND Corporation, PE-305-OSD, 2018; Arthur S. Hulnick, "Openness: Being Public About Secret Intelligence," *International Journal of Intelligence and CounterIntelligence*, Vol. 12, No. 4, 1999.

[3] Jeffrey A. Friedman and Richard Zeckhauser, "Why Assessing Estimative Accuracy Is Feasible and Desirable," *Intelligence and National Security*, Vol. 31, No. 2, 2016; Katrina Mulligan, Matt Olsen, and Alexandra Schmitt, "What the Intelligence Community Doesn't Know Is Hurting the United States," Center for American Progress, webpage, September 18, 2020.

[4] Kenneth G. Lieberthal, "The U.S. Intelligence Community and Foreign Policy: Getting Analysis Right," Brookings Institution blog, September 15, 2009.

[5] Uri Bar-Joseph, 2013.

[6] Intelligence Community Directive 203, 2015.

[7] Richards J. Heuer, Jr., *Psychology of Intelligence Analysis*, Langley, Va.: Central Intelligence Agency, Center for the Study of Intelligence, 1999.

[8] Gregory F. Treverton and C. Bryan Gabbard, *Assessing the Tradecraft of Intelligence Analysis*, Santa Monica, Calif.: RAND Corporation, TR-293, 2008.

9/11 Commission report,[9] an article on the Church Committee,[10] a book of ten cases of intelligence failures,[11] the IC Analytic Ombudsman report on politicization of intelligence on election interference,[12] a book discussing both intelligence failures and successes,[13] and a book discussing the Iraq WMD NIE and the Iran NIE.[14] The fourth theme included related studies and commentary. Issues discussed on this theme include selective declassification,[15] public support for the IC,[16] tension over citizens' privacy and security, President Trump's politicization of the IC,[17] the threat posed by degrading public trust in government,[18] institutional bias or politicization in the CIA,[19] and the proper role of the IC in society.[20]

---

[9] National Commission on Terrorist Attacks Upon the United States, *The 9/11 Commission Report*, Washington, D.C., 2004a.

[10] Loch K. Johnson, "Congressional Supervision of America's Secret Agencies: The Experience and Legacy of the Church Committee," *Public Administration Review*, Vol. 64, No. 1, January-February 2004.

[11] John Hughes-Wilson, *Military Intelligence Blunders and Cover-Ups*, New York: Carroll and Graf Publishers, 2004.

[12] ODNI, *Analytic Ombudsman Report on Politicization of Intelligence on Election Interference*, January 6, 2021.

[13] Jeffrey T. Richelson, *A Century of Spies: Intelligence in the Twentieth Century*, New York: Oxford University Press, 1995.

[14] Thomas Fingar, Reducing Uncertainty: Intelligence Analysis and National Security, Stanford, Calif.: Stanford University Press, 2011.

[15] Dudding, 2021.

[16] Steve Slick and Joshua Busby, "Support for U.S. Intelligence Continues, Despite Presidential Attacks and Concerns over Transparency," *Lawfare* blog, September 21, 2020.

[17] Morell, Haines, and Cohen, 2020.

[18] Ron Fournier, "Why We Can't Trust the NSA (and Why That's a Crisis)," *The Atlantic*, June 1, 2015; Stephen Slick, "This November, America's Safety Is on the Ballot," *Foreign Policy*, October 9, 2020.

[19] Gentry, 2018.

[20] Jeff Rogg, "The U.S. Intelligence Community's 'MacArthur Moment,'" *International Journal of Intelligence and CounterIntelligence*, Vol. 33, No. 4, 2020.

Systematic Literature Review

In Table C.1, we display the search strings that we used to identify articles in two databases of peer-reviewed journal articles, Scopus and Web of Science. For both databases, we used a broad set of terms that included public opinion, trust, mistrust, politicization, and partisanship. Given the overlap of terms related to the IC and other irrelevant topics (e.g., Intelligence Quotient or artificial intelligence), we developed two search terms for each database. The first focused on specific target journals that we identified during our exploratory literature review (e.g., *Journal of Intelligence and Counter-Intelligence*). The second search string relaxed this constraint to focus not on the journal but on titles that related to the IC (e.g., "intelligence profession" or "intelligence work"). We searched for relevant articles from 1979 to 2021, with the earliest article in our sample published in 1988.[21]

Our search strings resulted in a total of 211 articles in our sample. Next, a research assistant on the team reviewed the titles, abstracts, and some of the main text of these articles to identify which ones were relevant to trust and the IC. Using the results of this review, we identified 51 articles representing 24.2 percent of our total sample. We then organized these articles by time they were published and prioritized them by their citation counts.[22] We focused our attention on articles in our sample that had more citations.

Our sample of articles is not representative of all research on the IC for at least three reasons. First, our search strings likely captured only a subset of articles on trust in the IC. We developed this string after our exploratory literature review with the help of a research librarian. The goal was to identify a broad cross-section of articles that encompass not only the analysis and collection of intelligence but also public views of this process. Put simply, we sacrificed breadth for depth in our sample. Second, most of our articles are restricted to two major databases (Scopus and Web of Science). Research

---

[21] Given the nonpublic nature of work in the IC, some articles in our sample were published well after the events studied.

[22] We used Google Scholar to estimate citation counts as of May 2021. While they are imperfect, citation counts highlight which articles are influential under the assumption that others are citing the article because it is relevant to current work. This estimate does not exclude self-citations, however.

on the IC is a specialty field, and not all journals from this field are indexed in our databases (e.g., CIA's *Studies in Intelligence*). Third, we focused on English-language research that focused primarily on the IC, not the intelligence communities of our allies or adversaries.

TABLE C.1

Search Strings and Number of Articles Retrieved in Scopus and Web of Science, 1979–2021

Database Name	Search String	Articles Retrieved
Scopus	(TITLE-ABS-KEY ("public opinion" OR "public trust" OR "public criticism" OR mistrust* OR distrust* OR reputation* OR skeptic* OR politics* OR politiciz* OR partisan*)) AND (SRCTITLE ("defense intelligence journal" OR "journal of strategic studies" OR "journal of intelligence history" OR "journal of intelligence and counterintelligence" OR "studies in intelligence" OR "intelligence and national security"))	94
	TITLE-ABS-KEY ("public opinion" OR "public trust" OR mistrust* OR distrust* OR reputation* OR criticism OR skeptic* OR politics* OR politiciz* OR partisan*) AND TITLE-ABS-KEY ("intelligence community" OR "intelligence agen*" OR "intelligence profession*" OR "intelligence work*")	88
Web of Science	TOPIC: ("public opinion" OR "attitudes and opinion*" OR "public trust" OR "public criticism" OR mistrust* OR distrust* OR reputation* OR skeptic* OR politics* OR politiciz* OR partisan*) AND SO = ("intelligence and national security") OR SO = ("journal of intelligence and counterintelligence") OR SO = ("journal of intelligence history") OR SO = ("defense intelligence journal") OR SO = ("journal of strategic studies") OR SO = ("studies in intelligence")	14
	ts = ("public opinion" OR "attitudes and opinion*" OR "public trust" OR "public criticism" OR mistrust* OR distrust* OR reputation* OR skeptic* OR politics* OR politiciz* OR partisan*) AND ts = ("intelligence community" Or "intelligence profession*" OR "intelligence agen*" OR "intelligence work*")	15
Total		211

Abbreviations

9/11	September 11, 2001, terrorist attacks
ABM	anti-ballistic missile
CENTCOM	U.S. Central Command
CIA	Central Intelligence Agency
COCOM	combatant command
COVID-19	coronavirus disease 2019
DCI	Director of Central Intelligence
DDI	Deputy Director of Intelligence
DIA	Defense Intelligence Agency
DNI	Director of National Intelligence
DoD	U.S. Department of Defense
FBI	Federal Bureau of Investigation
IC	U.S. Intelligence Community
ICBM	intercontinental ballistic missile
IG	inspector general
ISF	Iraqi Security Forces
ISIL	Islamic State of Iraq and the Levant
ISIS	Islamic State of Iraq and Syria
JTF	Joint Task Force
MACV	U.S. Military Assistance Command, Vietnam
MIRV	multiple independent reentry vehicle
NIE	National Intelligence Estimate
NSA	National Security Agency
NSC	National Security Council
O/B	order of battle

ODNI	Office of the Director of National Intelligence
PCTEG	Policy Counter Terrorism Evaluation Group
PDB	President's Daily Brief
SNIE	Special National Intelligence Estimate
WMD	weapons of mass destruction

References

Adams, Sam, *War of Numbers: An Intelligence Memoir*, South Royalton, Vt.: Steerforth Press, 1994.

Artner, Stephen, Richard S. Girven, and James B. Bruce, *Assessing the Value of Structured Analytic Techniques in the U.S. Intelligence Community*, Santa Monica, Calif.: RAND Corporation, RR-1408-OSD, 2016. As of April 20, 2022: https://www.rand.org/pubs/research_reports/RR1408.html

Bar-Joseph, Uri, "The Politicization of Intelligence: A Comparative Study," *International Journal of Intelligence and CounterIntelligence*, Vol. 26, No. 2, 2013, pp. 347–369.

Bar-Joseph, Uri, and Jack S. Levy, "Conscious Action and Intelligence Failure," *Political Science Quarterly*, Vol. 124, No. 3, Fall 2009, pp. 461–488.

Bar-Joseph, Uri, and Rose McDermott, *Intelligence Success and Failure: The Human Factor*, New York: Oxford University Press, 2017.

Barnes, Julian E., Nicholas Fandos, and Adam Goldman, "Republican Senators Are Cool to Trump's Choice for Top Intelligence Post," *New York Times*, July 29, 2019.

Barnes, Julian E., and Adam Goldman, "John Ratcliffe Pledged to Stay Apolitical. Then He Began Serving Trump's Political Agenda," *New York Times*, October 9, 2020.

Barnes, Julian E., Adam Goldman, and Nicholas Fandos, "Richard Grenell Begins Overhauling Intelligence Office, Prompting Fears of Partisanship," *New York Times*, February 21, 2020.

Beavers, Olivia, "Trump Blasts Intel Chiefs as 'Passive and Naïve,'" *The Hill*, January 30, 2019.

Betts, Richard K., "Analysis, War, and Decision: Why Intelligence Failures Are Inevitable," *World Politics*, Vol. 31, No. 1, October 1978, pp. 61–89.

Betts, Richard K., "Two Faces of Intelligence Failure: September 11 and Iraq's Missing WMD," *Political Science Quarterly*, Vol. 122, No. 4, Winter 2007/2008, pp. 585–606.

Bissell, Richard M., Jr., *Reflections of a Cold Warrior: From Yalta to the Bay of Pigs*, New Haven, Conn.: Yale University Press, 1996.

Blumenthal, Sidney, "Spies Toed Iraq Line, or Fell to the Hawks," *Sydney Morning Herald*, February 9, 2004.

Bruce, James B., Sina Beaghley, and W. George Jameson, *Secrecy in U.S. National Security: Why a Paradigm Shift Is Needed*, Santa Monica, Calif.: RAND Corporation, PE-305-OSD, 2018. As of March 30, 2022: https://www.rand.org/pubs/perspectives/PE305.html

Bush, George W., "Address Before a Joint Session of the Congress on the State of the Union," January 28, 2003.

CBS News and *New York Times*, "Poll: Obama and the Republicans in Congress/Gun Control/Syria," version 2, data set, Ithaca, N.Y.: Cornell University, Roper Center for Public Opinion Research, 2013.

Center for the Study of Intelligence, *"Our First Line of Defense": Presidential Reflections on US Intelligence*, Washington, D.C., 1996.

Chan, Steve, "The Intelligence of Stupidity: Understanding Failures in Strategic Warning," *American Political Science Review*, Vol. 73, No. 1, March 1979, pp. 171–180.

Clarke, Richard A., *Against All Enemies: Inside America's War on Terror*, New York: Free Press, 2004.

Conway, Patrick, "Red Team: How the Neoconservatives Helped Cause the Iraq Intelligence Failure," *Intelligence and National Security*, Vol. 27, No. 4, August 2012, pp. 488–512.

Dahl, Erik J., *Intelligence and Surprise Attack: Failure and Success from Pearl Harbor to 9/11 and Beyond*, Washington, D.C.: Georgetown University Press, 2013.

Davies, Philip H. J., "Intelligence Culture and Intelligence Failure in Britain and the United States," *Cambridge Review of International Affairs*, Vol. 17, No. 3, 2004, pp. 495–520.

Davis, Jack, "Why Bad Things Happen to Good Analysts," *Studies in Intelligence*, Vol. 60, No. 3, September 2016, pp. 14–24.

Diamond, Jeremy, Evan Perez, Pamela Brown, and Jim Sciutto, "Trump Derides Intel Briefing on 'So-Called' Russian Hacking," CNN, January 4, 2017.

Dilanian, Ken, "Intel Officials Worry Trump's Pick for Top Spy Will Politicize the Job," NBC News, July 29, 2019.

Draper, Robert, "Unwanted Truths: Inside Trump's Battle with U.S. Intelligence Agencies," *New York Times*, August 25, 2020.

Dreyfuss, Robert, "The Pentagon Muzzles the CIA," *American Prospect*, November 21, 2002.

Dudding, Sasha, "Spinning Secrets: The Dangers of Selective Declassification," *Yale Law Journal*, Vol. 130, No. 3, January 2021, pp. 708–777.

Erickson, Pete, Seth Loertscher, David C. Lane, and Paul Erickson, "Twenty Years After the USS Cole Attack: The Search for Justice," *Combating Terrorism Center Sentinel*, Vol. 13, No. 10, October 2020, pp. 46–54.

FBI—*See* Federal Bureau of Investigation.

Federal Bureau of Investigation, "History: Famous Cases and Criminals—Aldrich Ames," webpage, undated a. As of January 31, 2022:
https://www.fbi.gov/history/famous-cases/aldrich-ames

Federal Bureau of Investigation, "History: Famous Cases and Criminals—Robert Hanssen," webpage, undated b. As of January 31, 2022:
https://www.fbi.gov/history/famous-cases/robert-hanssen

Federal Bureau of Investigation, "History: Famous Cases and Criminals—USS Cole Bombing," webpage, undated c. As of January 31, 2022:
https://www.fbi.gov/history/famous-cases/uss-cole-bombing

Fingar, Thomas, *Reducing Uncertainty: Intelligence Analysis and National Security*, Stanford, Calif.: Stanford University Press, 2011.

Fleischer, Ari, "Press Briefing by Ari Fleischer," The American Presidency Project, October 9, 2002. As of January 4, 2022:
https://www.presidency.ucsb.edu/node/272038

Ford, Harold P., *CIA and the Vietnam Policymakers: Three Episodes 1962–1968*, Langley, Va.: Central Intelligence Agency, Center for the Study of Intelligence, 1998.

Fournier, Ron, "Why We Can't Trust the NSA (and Why That's a Crisis)," *The Atlantic*, June 1, 2015.

Fox News, "Poll: Obama/Sarah Palin/Economy/Osama bin Laden," version 2, data set, Ithaca, N.Y.: Cornell University, Roper Center for Public Opinion Research, August 2011.

Fox News, "Poll: Obama/Health Care/Privacy," version 2, data set, Ithaca, N.Y.: Cornell University, Roper Center for Public Opinion Research, November 2013.

Freedman, Lawrence, *U.S. Intelligence and the Soviet Strategic Threat*, Princeton, N.J.: Princeton University Press, 1977.

Freeh, Louis J., *My FBI: Bringing Down the Mafia, Investigating Bill Clinton, and Fighting the War on Terror*, New York: St. Martin's Press, 2005.

Friedman, Jeffrey A., and Richard Zeckhauser, "Why Assessing Estimative Accuracy Is Feasible and Desirable," *Intelligence and National Security*, Vol. 31, No. 2, 2016, pp. 178–200.

Gallup, "Gallup Daily: Obama Job Approval," webpage, undated. As of September 23, 2021:
https://news.gallup.com/poll/113980/Gallup-Daily-Obama-Job-Approval.aspx

Gentry, John A., "Intelligence Analyst/Manager Relations at the CIA," *Intelligence and National Security*, Vol. 10, No. 4, 1995, pp. 133–146.

Gentry, John A., "Intelligence Failure Reframed," *Political Science Quarterly*, Vol. 123, No. 2, Summer 2008, pp. 247–270.

Gentry, John A., "A New Form of Politicization? Has the CIA Become Institutionally Biased or Politicized?" *International Journal of Intelligence and CounterIntelligence*, Vol. 31, No. 4, 2018, pp. 647–680.

Gentry, John A., "Partisan Political Polemics: Wrecking One's Reputation," *International Journal of Intelligence and CounterIntelligence*, Vol. 32, No. 1, 2019a, pp. 170–178.

Gentry, John A., "'Truth' as a Tool of the Politicization of Intelligence," *International Journal of Intelligence and CounterIntelligence*, Vol. 32, No. 2, 2019b, pp. 217–247.

Gittens, Hasani, and Ken Dilanian, "Trump Takes Jab at 'Intelligence' Officials for Allegedly Delaying 'Russian Hacking' Briefing," NBC News, January 4, 2017.

Gordon, Michael R., "Threats and Responses: Intelligence—U.S. Aides Split on Assessment of Iraq's Plans," *New York Times*, October 10, 2002.

Graff, Garrett M., "Trump's New Intelligence Chief Spells Trouble," *Wired*, May 26, 2020.

Handel, Michael, "The Politics of Intelligence," *Intelligence and National Security*, Vol. 2, No. 4, 1987, pp. 5–46.

Handel, Michael I., *War, Strategy, and Intelligence*, New York: Frank Cass and Company, 1989.

Harris, Shane, "DNI Ratcliffe Has Broken His Promise to Keep Politics out of Intelligence, Intelligence Veterans Say," *Washington Post*, October 8, 2020.

Helgerson, John L., *Getting to Know the President, Second Edition: Intelligence Briefings of Presidential Candidates, 1952–2004*, Langley, Va.: Central Intelligence Agency, Center for the Study of Intelligence, 2012.

Helms, Richard, *A Look over My Shoulder: A Life in the Central Intelligence Agency*, New York: Random House, 2003.

Heuer, Richards J., Jr., *Psychology of Intelligence Analysis*, Langley, Va.: Central Intelligence Agency, Center for the Study of Intelligence, 1999.

Hughes-Wilson, John, *Military Intelligence Blunders and Cover-Ups*, New York: Carroll and Graf Publishers, 2004.

Hulnick, Arthur S., "Openness: Being Public About Secret Intelligence," *International Journal of Intelligence and CounterIntelligence*, Vol. 12, No. 4, 1999, pp. 463–483.

Intelligence Community Directive 203, *Analytic Standards*, Office of the Director of National Intelligence, January 2, 2015.

"'Intelligence Matters' Host Michael Morell on the Top Global Threats in 2022," CBS News, updated January 6, 2022.

Isikoff, Michael, "U.S. Failure to Retaliate for USS Cole Attack Rankled Then—and Now," NBC News, October 12, 2010.

Isikoff, Michael, and David Corn, *Hubris: The Inside Story of Spin, Scandal, and the Selling of the Iraq War*, New York: Three Rivers Press, 2006.

Ignatius, David, "CIA Documents Supported Susan Rice's Description of Benghazi Attacks," *Washington Post*, October 19, 2012.

Jalonick, Mary Clare, and Eric Tucker, "Divided Senate Confirms Ratcliffe as Intelligence Chief," AP News, May 21, 2020.

Jensen, Mark A., "Intelligence Failures: What Are They Really and What Do We Do About Them?" *Intelligence and National Security*, Vol. 27, No. 2, 2012, pp. 261–282.

Jervis, Robert, *Why Intelligence Fails: Lessons from the Iranian Revolution and the Iraq War*, Ithaca, N.Y.: Cornell University Press, 2010a.

Jervis, Robert, "Why Intelligence and Policymakers Clash," *Political Science Quarterly*, Vol. 125, No. 2, Summer 2010b, pp. 185–204.

Jervis, Robert, "Introduction by Robert Jervis, Columbia University: Roundtable 10-15 on *Intelligence Success and Failure: The Human Factor*," H-Diplo, *International Security Studies Forum Roundtable*, Vol. 10, No. 15, June 4, 2018. As of January 8, 2022: https://issforum.org/roundtables/10-15-human-factor#_Toc515746264

Jervis, Robert, Richard Ned Lebow, and Janice Gross Stein, *Psychology and Deterrence*, Baltimore, Md.: Johns Hopkins University Press, 1985.

Johnson, Loch K., "Congressional Supervision of America's Secret Agencies: The Experience and Legacy of the Church Committee," *Public Administration Review*, Vol. 64, No. 1, January-February 2004, pp. 3–14.

Jones, Christopher M., "The CIA Under Clinton: Continuity and Change," *International Journal of Intelligence and CounterIntelligence*, Vol. 14, No. 4, 2001, pp. 503–528.

Kelly, Mary Louise, "A History of Trump's Broken Ties to the U.S. Intelligence Community," *All Things Considered*, October 28, 2019.

Knorr, Klaus, "Failures in National Intelligence Estimates: The Case of the Cuban Missiles," *World Politics*, Vol. 16, No. 3, April 1964, pp. 455–467.

Kuhns, Woodrow J., "Intelligence Failures: Forecasting and the Lessons of Epistemology," in Richard K. Betts and Thomas G. Mahnken, eds., *Paradoxes of Strategic Intelligence: Essays in Honor of Michael I. Handel*, London: Routledge, 2003, pp. 80–100.

Lepri, Charlotte, "Obama's Intelligence Policy: Meeting New Challenges," in Bahram M. Rajaee and Mark J. Miller, eds., *National Security Under the Obama Administration*, New York: Palgrave Macmillan, 2012, pp. 63–80.

Lieberthal, Kenneth G., "The U.S. Intelligence Community and Foreign Policy: Getting Analysis Right," Brookings Institution blog, September 15, 2009. As of April 20, 2022:
https://www.brookings.edu/research/
the-u-s-intelligence-community-and-foreign-policy-getting-analysis-right

Marrin, Stephen, "The 9/11 Terrorist Attacks: A Failure of Policy Not Strategic Intelligence Analysis," *Intelligence and National Security*, Vol. 26, Nos. 2-3, 2011, pp. 182–202.

McGarr, Paul, "'Do We Still Need the CIA?' Daniel Patrick Moynihan, the Central Intelligence Agency and U.S. Foreign Policy," *History*, Vol. 100, No. 2, April 2015, pp. 275–292.

Moran, Christopher R., and Richard J. Aldrich, "Trump and the CIA: Borrowing from Nixon's Playbook," *Foreign Affairs*, April 24, 2017.

Morell, Michael, Avril Haines, and David S. Cohen, "Trump's Politicization of U.S. Intelligence Agencies Could End in Disaster," *Foreign Policy*, April 28, 2020.

Morell, Michael, and Bill Harlow, *The Great War of Our Time: The CIA's Fight Against Terrorism—from Al Qa'ida to ISIS*, New York: Grand Central Publishing, 2015.

Moynihan, Daniel P., "Opinion: Do We Still Need the C.I.A.? The State Dept. Can Do the Job," *New York Times*, May 19, 1991.

Mufson, Steven, "Clinton to Send Message with Economic Choices," *Washington Post*, November 8, 1992.

Mulligan, Katrina, Matt Olsen, and Alexandra Schmitt, "What the Intelligence Community Doesn't Know Is Hurting the United States," Center for American Progress, webpage, September 18, 2020. As of November 19, 2020:
https://www.americanprogress.org/issues/security/reports/2020/09/18/490532/
intelligence-community-doesnt-know-hurting-united-states

Myleftnutmegblog, "Gen. Eric Shinseki from 02.25.03," video, YouTube, December 7, 2008. As of January 4, 2022:
https://youtu.be/a_xchyIeCQw

National Commission on Terrorist Attacks Upon the United States, *The 9/11 Commission Report*, Washington, D.C., 2004a.

National Commission on Terrorist Attacks Upon the United States, *The 9/11 Commission Report: Final Report of the National Commission on Terrorist Attacks Upon the United States—Executive Summary*, Washington, D.C., 2004b.

Nixon, Richard, "The President's News Conference," American Presidency Project, April 18, 1969a. As of January 4, 2022:
https://www.presidency.ucsb.edu/node/238866/

Nixon, Richard, "The President's News Conference," American Presidency Project, June 19, 1969b. As of January 4, 2022:
https://www.presidency.ucsb.edu/documents/
the-presidents-news-conference-150

O'Donnell, Patrick K., *Operatives, Spies, and Saboteurs: The Unknown Story of the Men and Women of WWII's OSS*, New York: Citadel Press Books, 2004.

ODNI—*See* Office of the Director of National Intelligence.

Office of the Director of National Intelligence, "Bin Laden's Bookshelf," webpage, undated a. As of September 22, 2021:
https://www.odni.gov/index.php/features/bin-laden-s-bookshelf

Office of the Director of National Intelligence, "Objectivity," webpage, undated b. As of January 7, 2022:
https://www.dni.gov/index.php/how-we-work/objectivity

Office of the Director of National Intelligence, "Principles of Professional Ethics for the Intelligence Community," webpage, undated c. As of January 4, 2022:
https://www.dni.gov/index.php/who-we-are/organizations/clpt/
clpt-related-menus/clpt-related-links/ic-principles-of-professional-ethics

Office of the Director of National Intelligence, "Statement by the Director of Public Affairs for ODNI, Shawn Turner, on the Intelligence Related to the Terrorist Attack on the U.S. Consulate in Benghazi, Libya," press release, September 28, 2012.

Office of the Director of National Intelligence, "Benghazi Emails on Unclassified Talking Points," May 29, 2013.

Office of the Director of National Intelligence, "(U) Selected CENTCOM Respondent Descriptions from the FY2015 AOPS," October 17, 2016.

Office of the Director of National Intelligence, *Analytic Ombudsman Report on Politicization of Intelligence on Election Interference*, January 6, 2021.

Office of the Press Secretary, "Press Briefing by Press Secretary Jay Carney, 5/4/2011," Washington, D.C.: Obama White House Archives, May 4, 2011. As of September 22, 2021:
https://obamawhitehouse.archives.gov/the-press-office/2011/05/04/
press-briefing-press-secretary-jay-carney-542011

Office of the Press Secretary, "Press Briefing by Press Secretary Jay Carney, 5/3/12," Washington, D.C.: Obama White House Archives, May 3, 2012. As of September 22, 2021:
https://obamawhitehouse.archives.gov/the-press-office/2012/05/03/
press-briefing-press-secretary-jay-carney-5312

Office of the Press Secretary, "Press Briefing by Press Secretary Josh Earnest, 12/8/16," Washington, D.C.: Obama White House Archives, December 8, 2016. As of September 8, 2021:
https://obamawhitehouse.archives.gov/the-press-office/2016/12/08/
press-briefing-press-secretary-josh-earnest-12816

Packer, George, *The Assassins' Gate: America in Iraq*, New York: Farrar, Straus and Giroux, 2005.

"Panetta: Job of Intel Community Is to Speak Truth to Power," CNN, video, January 31, 2019. As of January 4, 2022:
https://www.cnn.com/videos/politics/2019/01/31/donald-trump-intel-chiefs-
dan-coats-leon-panetta-sot-ac-vpx.cnn

Pillar, Paul R., *Intelligence and U.S. Foreign Policy: Iraq, 9/11, and Misguided Reform*, New York: Columbia University Press, 2011.

Priess, David, *The President's Book of Secrets: The Untold Story of Intelligence Briefings to America's Presidents from Kennedy to Obama*, New York: PublicAffairs, 2016.

Quinn, Melissa, "The Internal Watchdogs Trump Has Fired or Replaced," CBS News, May 19, 2020. As of April 1, 2022:
https://www.cbsnews.com/news/
trump-inspectors-general-internal-watchdogs-fired-list

Rand, Emily, "Source: 2.7 Terabytes of Data Recovered from Bin Laden Compound," CBS News, May 6, 2011. As of September 23, 2021:
https://www.cbsnews.com/news/
source-27-terabytes-of-data-recovered-from-bin-laden-compound

Richelson, Jeffrey T., *A Century of Spies: Intelligence in the Twentieth Century*, New York: Oxford University Press, 1995.

Ricks, Thomas E., "Iraq War Planner Downplays Role," *Washington Post*, October 22, 2003.

Riley, Russell L., "Bill Clinton: Domestic Affairs," University of Virginia Miller Center, webpage, undated. As of April 1, 2022: https://millercenter.org/president/clinton/domestic-affairs

Risen, James, "The Nation; The Clinton Administration's See-No-Evil C.I.A," *New York Times*, September 10, 2000.

Robert James Woolsey, interview, Charlottesville, Va.: University of Virginia, Miller Center, William J. Clinton Presidential History Project, January 13, 2010.

Rogg, Jeff, "The U.S. Intelligence Community's 'MacArthur Moment,'" *International Journal of Intelligence and CounterIntelligence*, Vol. 33, No. 4, 2020, pp. 666–681.

Rosenberg, Matthew, "In Osama Bin Laden Library: Illuminati and Bob Woodward," *New York Times*, May 20, 2015.

Rovner, Joshua, *Fixing the Facts: National Security and the Politics of Intelligence*, Ithaca, N.Y.: Cornell University Press, 2011.

Schmitt, Eric, "Threats and Responses: Military Spending; Pentagon Contradicts General on Iraq Occupation Force's Size," *New York Times*, February 28, 2003.

Schulman, Daniel, "CIA Veteran: How Robert Gates Cooked the Intelligence," *Mother Jones*, December 4, 2006.

Shanker, Thom, "New Strategy Vindicates Ex-Army Chief Shinseki," *New York Times*, January 12, 2007.

Sheehan, Michael A., *Crush the Cell: How to Defeat Terrorism Without Terrorizing Ourselves*, New York: Three Rivers Press, 2008.

Silberman, Laurence H., and Charles S. Robb, *The Commission on the Intelligence Capabilities of the United States Regarding Weapons of Mass Destruction: Report to the President of the United States*, Washington, D.C., March 31, 2005.

Slick, Stephen, "This November, America's Safety Is on the Ballot," *Foreign Policy*, October 9, 2020.

Slick, Steve, and Joshua Busby, "Support for U.S. Intelligence Continues, Despite Presidential Attacks and Concerns over Transparency," *Lawfare* blog, September 21, 2020. As of September 29, 2020: https://www.lawfareblog.com/support-us-intelligence-continues-despite-presidential-attacks-and-concerns-over-transparency

Special National Intelligence Estimate 14.3-67, *Capabilities of the Vietnamese Communists for Fighting in South Vietnam*, Washington, D.C.: Central Intelligence Agency, Office of National Estimates, November 13, 1967.

SNIE—*See* Special National Intelligence Estimate.

Steinberg, James B., "The Policymaker's Perspective: Transparency and Partnership," in Roger Z. George and James B. Bruce, eds., *Analyzing Intelligence: National Security Practitioners' Perspectives*, 2nd ed., Washington, D.C.: Georgetown University Press, 2014, pp. 93–101.

Sterling, Claire, *The Terror Network: The Secret War of International Terrorism*, New York: Henry Colt and Company, 1981.

Stimson, Henry L., and McGeorge Bundy, *On Active Services in Peace and War*, New York: Hippocrene Books, 1971.

Suskind, Ron, *The One Percent Doctrine: Deep Inside America's Pursuit of Its Enemies Since 9/11*, New York: Simon and Schuster, 2006.

Tenet, George, and Bill Harlow, *At the Center of the Storm: My Years at the CIA*, New York: HarperCollins Publishers, 2007.

Tetlock, Philip E., and Barbara A. Mellers, "Intelligent Management of Intelligence Agencies: Beyond Accountability Ping-Pong," *American Psychologist*, Vol. 66, No. 6, 2011, pp. 542–554.

Treverton, Gregory F., and C. Bryan Gabbard, *Assessing the Tradecraft of Intelligence Analysis*, Santa Monica, Calif.: RAND Corporation, TR-293, 2008. As of April 20, 2022:
https://www.rand.org/pubs/technical_reports/TR293.html

Troyan, Mary, "House Benghazi Committee Files Final Report and Shuts Down," *USA Today*, December 12, 2016.

"Trump CIA Speech Transcript," CBS News, January 23, 2017.

Turner, Stansfield, *Burn Before Reading: Presidents, CIA Directors, and Secret Intelligence*, New York: Hyperion Books, 2006.

Tuttle, Ian, "House Intel Investigation on Benghazi Clears Administration, Intelligence Community of Wrongdoing," *National Review*, November 21, 2014.

U.S. Code, Title 50, Section 3023, Director of National Intelligence.

U.S. Department of State, Office of the Historian, "The Bay of Pigs Invasion and Its Aftermath, April 1961–October 1962," *Milestones in the History of U.S. Foreign Relations: 1961–1968*, undated.

U.S. House of Representatives, *(U) Initial Findings of the U.S. House of Representatives Joint Task Force on U.S. Central Command Intelligence Analysis*, Washington, D.C., August 10, 2016.

U.S. House and U.S. Senate Joint Intelligence Committee, "Written Statement for the Record of the Director of Central Intelligence Before the Joint Inquiry Committee," October 17, 2002.

U.S. Senate, *Intelligence and the ABM: Hearings Before the Committee on Foreign Relations*, Washington, D.C.: U.S. Government Printing Office, June 23, 1969.

U.S. Senate Select Committee on Intelligence, *An Assessment of the Aldrich H. Ames Espionage Case and Its Implications for U.S. Intelligence*, Washington, D.C.: U.S. Government Printing Office, November 1, 1994.

U.S. Senate Select Committee on Intelligence, "Senate Intelligence Committee Releases Declassified Bipartisan Report on Benghazi Terrorist Attacks," press release, January 15, 2014.

Wagner, John, and Greg Miller, "Trump Alleges Delay in His Briefing on 'So-Called' Russian Hacking; U.S. Official Says There Wasn't One," *Washington Post*, January 4, 2017.

Weiner, Tim, *Legacy of Ashes: The History of the CIA*, New York: Doubleday, 2007.

Wheaton, Kristan J., "Evaluating Intelligence: Answering Questions Asked and Not," *International Journal of Intelligence and CounterIntelligence*, Vol. 22, No. 4, 2009, pp. 614–631.

Whipple, Chris, *The Spymasters: How the CIA Directors Shape History and the Future*, New York: Scribner, 2020.

Wohlstetter, Roberta, *Pearl Harbor: Warning and Decision*, Stanford, Calif.: Stanford University Press, 1962.

Zegart, Amy B., "September 11 and the Adaptation Failure of U.S. Intelligence Agencies," *International Security*, Vol. 29, No. 4, Spring 2005, pp. 78–111.